the
DIVINE
PRACTICE
of

ANGEL
NUMBERS

About the Author

Leeza Robertson is the author of *Tarot Court Cards for Beginners* and *Tarot Reversals for Beginners*, and she's the creator of two tarot decks: the *Mermaid Tarot* and *Animal Totem Tarot*. When she doesn't have her nose inside a book or her fingers dancing across a deck of cards, she runs her online class with her business partner, Pamela Chen. Together they are the Head Witches at the High Vibe Tarot Academy, which you can find at bit.ly /uftamagic.

the
DIVINE
PRACTICE
of
ANGEL
NUMBERS

Raise Your Vibration
with the
Archangels

555
777
999
111
333
222
888
666
444

Llewellyn Publications
Woodbury, Minnesota

1010

LEEZA ROBERTSON

1212

FIRST EDITION
First Printing, 2021

Book design by Samantha Peterson
Chakra figure on page 23 by Mary Ann Zapalac
Cover design by Shira Atakpu

Llewellyn Publications is a registered trademark of Llewellyn Worldwide Ltd.

Library of Congress Cataloging-in-Publication Data
Names: Robertson, Leeza, author.
Title: The divine practice of angel numbers : raise your vibration with the
    archangels / Leeza Robertson.
Description: First edition. | Woodbury, Minnesota : Llewellyn Publications,
    2021. | Summary: "Divine Practice of Angel Numbers shows how angels use
    special numbers to connect with you and teach specific ascension energy
    lessons. The book contains in-depth descriptions of thirteen archangels
    and thirteen numbers, each of which indicate a special lesson that the
    angels are lovingly sending. Their lessons are focused on spiritual and
    emotional milestones like letting go, becoming more comfortable with
    change, connecting with twin flame energy, moving beyond the ego, and
    many more. Each number has a short affirmation-style message from the
    angel, a deeper message, a description of the angel, a visualization or
    meditation, an angel connection prayer and automatic writing prompt, and
    an exercise for putting the number's energy into the suggested
    crystal"—Provided by publisher.
Identifiers: LCCN 2021014626 (print) | LCCN 2021014627 (ebook) | ISBN
    9780738766713 (paperback) | ISBN 9780738766843 (ebook)
Subjects: LCSH: Angels—Miscellanea. | Archangels—Miscellanea. | Symbolism
    of numbers.
Classification: LCC BF1623.A53 R63 2021 (print) | LCC BF1623.A53 (ebook)
    | DDC 235/.3—dc23
LC record available at https://lccn.loc.gov/2021014626
LC ebook record available at https://lccn.loc.gov/2021014627

Llewellyn Worldwide Ltd. does not participate in, endorse, or have any authority or responsibility concerning private business transactions between our authors and the public.

All mail addressed to the author is forwarded but the publisher cannot, unless specifically instructed by the author, give out an address or phone number.

Any internet references contained in this work are current at publication time, but the publisher cannot guarantee that a specific location will continue to be maintained. Please refer to the publisher's website for links to authors' websites and other sources.

Llewellyn Publications
A Division of Llewellyn Worldwide Ltd.
2143 Wooddale Drive
Woodbury, MN 55125-2989
www.llewellyn.com

Printed in the United States of America

Other Books by Leeza Robertson

Animal Totem Tarot

Mermaid Tarot

Pathworking the Tarot

Tarot Court Cards for Beginners

Tarot Reversals for Beginners

*This book is for all those who look down and
find nothing but feathers guiding them on their way.*

CONTENTS

ACKNOWLEDGMENTS

It takes a village to put a book into the marketplace, and this book would never have seen the light of day without my little village. Thank you to all the Llewellyn staff who made this book what it is today, with special thanks to Angela Wix for taking a chance on me. A huge thank you to my editor, Laure, who takes my raw words and polishes them to become sparkling gems. Most importantly, thank you, dear readers, because without you buying my books, I would not be able to keep writing them. And a heartfelt thanks to my wife, who is my biggest cheerleader and constant support person.

DISCLAIMER

This book is not intended to provide medical, legal, or mental health advice or to take the place of advice and treatment from your primary care provider. Readers are advised to consult their doctors or other qualified healthcare professionals regarding the treatment of their medical or mental health problems. Neither the publisher nor the author take any responsibility for any possible consequences from any treatment to any person reading or following the information in this book.

INTRODUCTION

Have you ever heard the joke about the woman who walks into her kitchen to find twelve archangels making sandwiches? Yeah, me neither, because it wasn't a joke, and that woman was me. I remember that 2009 spring morning like it was yesterday. I had been meditating and doing some healing work with a client when I walked into my kitchen and saw twelve angels making sandwiches. Archangel Uriel looked up from his sandwich making, smiled, waved, and said, "Hi," then proceeded to keep making his sandwich. When I first came across this gang of people in my kitchen, I thought someone had broken in. You see, they did not have wings or any markings to indicate they were indeed angels, nor were they see-through. They looked like regular everyday people. So I started yelling and looking for something to use as a weapon. Oddly enough Uriel had the sharpest knife I owned in his hand. Then I saw it: the glow and the light of their auras. I shut up and walked back to my room. I sat for a couple of minutes and walked back to the kitchen. No one was there. They had all gone, or so I thought, until Uriel tapped me on the shoulder and said, "We should talk."

It was the day I thought I had finally snapped. I honestly believed that I had lost my mind and slipped into a fantastic delusion to escape all of the pain I had refused to process in my life. Having been a student of the mind and psychoanalysis for over twenty years, I decided if I was going to go mad, the least I could do was document it and see what happened when my brain split into two. From a perverse giddy level, however, I was quite excited. Alas, my bubble was burst all too soon. As it turns out, I wasn't losing my grip on reality, which, to be honest, made what happened next, along with the next four months, more difficult to deal with. I wasn't wrong on the need to deal with my pain, though, and one of those twelve angels was about to take me to hell and back, and put it on repeat, until I dealt with that repressed pain. That angel was Archangel Uriel.

I started working with Uriel long before this particular physical incarnation, yet he has been here with me, during this turn of the sun, every step of the way. He has been there from my traumatic birth to my first brush with death at the age of five, through my abusive first marriage, and he even stood guard over me when I passed out drunk in a back alley in one of the suburbs of my home city of Melbourne, Australia. Uriel has been with me through it all, including the births of my three children. In all honesty, he is the reason I'm still standing. Whenever the wind was kicked out of me, he held me, dusted me off, and placed me lovingly back on my feet. Even though I have spent a good part of this particular incarnation oblivious to his presence, he has remained by my side, watched my back, and kept lifting me back up. That's love in its most pure and divine form. He is me and I am him; our energies are connected, whether I like it or not, and sometimes I don't like it. That's okay, though, because he doesn't care, complain, or get offended. He just always stays there. Yeah, he makes it very hard to ignore him.

I feel it is important to point something out right here at the beginning. Angels don't have a gender per se, and they aren't even physical. Though they sure do show up that way sometimes, they are just vibrational energy or aspects of Source energy. They come to us in a way that makes sense to us or in a way that aligns more cohesively with how we align to their vibrational energy. This is why Uriel presents as male energy to me. He is the most dominant male energy in my life; he shows up male, he feels male, and he has nothing but masculine love for me. However, not everyone will feel Uriel's vibes the same way. In fact, none of us feel the angels the same way, ever. It is one of the most interesting things about working with this energy we have named "angelic" because we all have very unique relationships with it and to it. What we believe, how we view the world, where we were born, and what spiritual practices we have all play a part in how we connect with angels. Now, I don't say that to ruffle your feathers or to say your beliefs are wrong. I am just opening the door for those who have yet to build a strong, safe, and stable relationship with the energy we call angels. If you are already working with the angels and you're feeling good with how you see, feel, and interact with them, fabulous, keep doing you! For those of you who are coming to this new, all I ask is that you stay open. Allow the angels to present themselves in a way that is most aligned to you. Don't worry if that's not what all the other books say, including this one. Just be receptive and allow the angels to guide you.

Uriel has in many ways been my gateway angel, and by that, I mean I started with him and then slowly worked my way into working with other angels. This may have been your experience as well. You may have found yourself more attracted to one angel over the others and through that angel, you moved on to explore what other angels you could work with. Whichever angel you feel the biggest pull to, or the one you see again and again, is your gateway angel. They are your guides to the new energy that is sweeping the planet, the new energy the angels call ascension energy. This energy has been building in momentum ever since we entered into the Age of Aquarius. Put simply, ascension energy is a new level of awareness. It is the angels' push to move us all into a state of awakening and to get us to step into our divine selves and start living life from a new, expanded perspective instead of the limited ego perspective we have been living during the Age of Pisces. Being willing to walk with the angels on this journey of ascension will not only benefit each of us as individuals—it will benefit the planet and all of humanity.

What You'll Find Here

The material in this book is just one of the many ways they—the angels—will teach you to be mindful of their presence and their ascension lessons. It is a way for them to open the door and let themselves into our lives slowly and gently. You could say it allows us to get a feel for them without having to make a real commitment to any angel in particular. This book is designed in a way that will allow you to be more mindful of the way angelic energy presents itself in your day-to-day life, as well as a way to introduce you to a few different angels. There are a total of thirteen angels in this book, and all of them "feel" different, have different messages, and have different lessons and guidance they can share with us if we allow them to.

Here is the list of angels you will meet throughout this book and the ascension lessons they are wanting to teach you:

- Archangel Metatron—Spinning infinite possibilities into your life.

- Archangel Michael—Dare to lead in a new age.

- Archangel Jophiel—Bring in twin flame energy to deepen your relationships.

- Archangel Haniel—Let your heart be the music for your ears.

- Archangel Samael—Shed the lens of the ego's limitation.

- Archangel Uriel—Let go and trust the change.

- Archangel Ariel—Love thyself as we love you.

- Archangel Raziel—The unknown is your guide; trust it.

- Archangel Raguel—You are currently in the flow of divine abundance.

- Archangel Raphiel—Healing energy is around you.

- Archangel Gabriel—You are one with everything.

- Archangel Sandalphon—Make a wish, the Universe is listening.

- Archangel Zadkiel—Use appreciation to expand into ascension.

Each of these angelic energies has aligned themselves with a set of numbers, and they have done this themselves; I did not order them. I merely asked them what lesson they wanted to teach, and that is where they were placed. I also asked them how they wanted to use the numbers in a way that was the most useful. This is why you will see we have mainly focused on triple number combinations. I am not the first person to use triple digits in relation to the angels, and I am pretty sure I will not be the last. I can't comment on how others have come up with their numbers, but the archangels and I have used numerology as our guide for this book, mainly because I personally use numerology as part of my spiritual practice. It is a number system I am familiar with and have been studying since 2007. You, however, don't need to know numerology to work with the numbers in this book. We just wanted to give you a little background on how these numbers came to be for our work together, especially when some of the numbers may represent a lesson you don't normally associate with it. Think of 666. Now, I know a lot of you have some personal beliefs around this number, none of which will match up with how we have talked about it in this book. This is because we—the angels and I—are using numerology as our message decoder. Sixes in numerology mean something specific, and that energy is amplified here in the 666 chapter.

You will not find every number combination in this book, but you will find the ones that are of most benefit to you, your life, and your ability to stay aligned to angelic ascension energy.

Here are the main numbers the angels want you to focus on with this book:

- 000—Everything is possible in this moment; all you have to do is spin my cube and see what portals of possibilities it opens.

- 111—It is time to step up, drop your resistance, and move into a heart-centered leadership role in one or more areas of your life.

- 222—You are being wrapped in the wings of Archangel Jophiel as she infuses you with healing twin flame energy.

- 333—The language of the heart is much more playful than most of the words you hear with your ears. Listen to the beats, groove with the rhythm, and dance your way to better-feeling vibes.

- 444—The ego is constantly focused on what it doesn't have or what might be taken from it, and this limits your vision, blinding you to the blessings of the Divine all around you.

- 555—Change is the only constant you will have in your physical experience, so make it your friend and invite it in.

- 666—Self-love is the greatest gift you can give yourself, for when you love yourself, you show the rest of the world how to love you as well.

- 777—When you open yourself up to things you don't know, you find more things to enrich and expand your life.

- 888—Stay in divine flow and understand the law of abundance in the physical world starts with you.

- 999—You are currently in the frequency of healing energy. Just relax, breathe, and allow the healing to wash over you.

- 1010—Learn the law of wholeness and understand your place in the universal matrix.

- 1111—You live in a friendly universe, and it wants to make all of your wishes come true. So make a wish, trust that it has been heard, and know that it is on its way back to you in the most perfect and divine way.

- 1212—Appreciation shifts your energy and aligns you with the frequencies of abundance. The more we find to appreciate, the more we manifest from a place of ascended awareness.

How to Use This Book

Within each of the angel number chapters, you will find:

- Message: A short affirmation-style message from the angel.

- Deeper Meaning: A deeper message about the number itself.

- The Angel: A section on the angel who volunteered to share information with you about the energy around that particular number and how they work with that energy to assist you.

- Visualization/Meditation: A meditation offered by the angel.

- Setting Up an Altar: How to set up an altar for your angel.

- Automatic Writing Prompts: An angel connection prayer and automatic writing prompts to further deepen your connection to the angels.

- Angel Crystal: Grounding the energy of the numbers and the angel into a crystal. A crystal will be listed along with an exercise on how to place that energy into your stone so you can carry it around with you.

- Additional Numbers: Each chapter will also have some additional number messages. These messages add to the energy of the main number, and they allow further dialogue and assistance from the angels you are working with in the chapter. These numbers come from the angels themselves, not from me personally; however, we have once again used basic numerology as our foundation for aligning messages to them.

Each chapter is designed as a complete stand-alone lesson for your number and its corresponding angel. This means you do not have to read this book cover to cover. You can instead jump in at any point and use the book as a form of divination. Let me give you an example. Hold the book close to your heart and take a few deep breaths, allowing yourself to relax into the moment, and let the breath work connect you to the book. Now ask, "Which angel would like me to be aware of their presence today?" and flip open the book. Whatever page you open to is the angel who wants to share your day with you. The number they are connected to will be the one you will be looking for throughout the day as an indicator that they are around. Read the message and deeper meaning and then put the book away. Carry on with your day mindfully and be aware of how and when your angel lets their presence be known.

Another way to use this book is to spend a couple of days tracking numbers you see. Just write them down and don't look for deeper meaning just yet. After three to four days, see which number or numbers you have seen the most. Now, go to that section in the book and see which angel has been trying to get your attention for the last couple of days. See what message they have been wanting to share with you and delve into the energy they have been aligning with you. Journal with the information you gather, ground that energy into your pocket crystal, and finish up with the connection meditation. You could also just do the prayer and devotion exercises if ritual is more your thing.

This book goes deeper into the numbers, deeper into the meanings, and aligns you to individual angels, so this simple work can go as far as you want it to go. The best part of this book is you don't have to wait to see the numbers to intentionally use them. You can draw on the numbers in this book anytime you want. Perhaps you want to work with one of the angels in this book, so you open up to that chapter and work your way through the different sections in that chapter. You can work on that chapter for as long as you wish. Want to work with Archangel Haniel? Go to chapter four, learn her numbers, get familiar with her signs, each day carry your crystal, and sink into her energy for as long as you feel called. This is the practice, the work, the living prayer that your life truly is. As you spend time with each of the angels and work with the numbers they provide, you will also create an angel story of your own. It will be one that you will have firsthand experience with. One that is personal, intimate, and true for you. The angels will guide you into your own sovereign state of being, and they will light your world, fill it with grace, and escort you along the path of awakening. As your energy shifts and life becomes lighter, you will be able to see the footprints of the angels everywhere you go. This is really the aim of any spiritual practice, and this one is no different. All you have to do is take the first step.

These are just a couple of ways to use this book. I am sure you will come up with many more fun ways to use the material offered in these pages. Just know there are no rules, only explorations and lessons in adventure, and the angels are all for adventure!

How to Connect with Angels as a Spiritual Practice

For the most part, people connect angels to religion. When one speaks of angels, it is not uncommon for people to presume you are religious or follow some form of religious practice. Generally speaking, this is where the average person first learns about these celestial beings, either in church or through some religious teaching or reading. I know that was true for me, having been brought up Catholic. It was this connection to religion and its dogma that made me reject my first couple of angel encounters. I didn't want any part of religion that, in my experience, had included very unfair gender biases and racist and homophobic beliefs. Religion, to me, was something that wanted people to all be the same and to follow its rules and code. It was going to send you to hell if you didn't do as it said. I associated angels as religious enforcers, the police of God, if you will. I wasn't the friendliest person when the celestials started to grace my life. I told them to fuck off at least one hundred times a day. I had grown up with a very negative story around who and what an angel was and what role they played in the order of the universe.

Uriel, however, never seemed to get the message. He just stayed. I told a friend about this, and she told me to hear the angels out, that perhaps they just had a message and would be on their way once their job was complete. So I caved with the hope that if I listened to what he/they had to say, the angels would go away. That didn't happen either. It took a long time for me to realize that I was the one holding all of the bias cards, not the angels. I had allowed human-made religious storytelling to tarnish my lens. I had to let go of everything I thought I knew about angels and be willing to learn again, but this time from the angels themselves. I had to drop my resistance to their so-called narratives and allow them to tell me their story, on their terms and in their own way.

This taught me a lot about agency and the power of telling one's own story. Much like the angels, many of us have allowed other people to tell stories about us. We have become characters in narratives that are sometimes very far removed from who we are. Bridging that gap between real self and character self would require someone else being willing to listen, really listen. So I gave the angels the chance to speak and to be heard, because at the end of the day, I would want others to do the same for me. I would hope that someone, somewhere, would be witness to my telling of my story. In many respects this is one of the ways the ascension numbers work (the number associated with each angel). They are part of that retelling. They are part of the story the angels wish to tell about themselves and you, even if they are using me as a vessel to be able to spread the story via this book.

This brings me to a very important point. Don't take my word for any of it. If at any time something in this book feels out of alignment with you, lean in and open yourself up to hear from the angels themselves. Allow them to speak to you in your words through your own personal beliefs. How they talk to you may be very different from how they talk to me. Just be open to listening, really listening.

I try very hard not to put my own personal beliefs or bias into their words. I have had to learn how to approach my work with them as a clear vessel and as part of a much larger spiritual practice. It hasn't been easy, and it is still very much a work in progress. It is one of the reasons it has taken me so long to sit down and write another book with them. I needed to know I was in the right place for this information to come through. The angels are always in the right headspace, always clear and always without bias. It is just we humans who need to get our heads on straight, which leads me to the use of the word "God"—or God/Source/Divine/Goddess—in this book. When the angels speak of God, they are not speaking of the one you were taught about in church. The God they speak of is an energy, a creative, inclusive energy that weaves itself through everything. There is nothing that God is not a part of. This took me a very long time to come to terms with, as I am a bit anti-God if I am being honest. So just as I have had to relearn the narrative of the angels, I, too, have had to relearn about God/Source/Divine/Goddess energy.

As you move through this book, you may find yourself having to let go of things you have learned. You may feel the pull to allow new information and a new story into your life. Things you thought you knew may no longer feel real anymore. This is perfectly normal when one starts this journey. It is why we ask you to not compare this book to any other book written on a similar subject. Instead, view them as companions, each telling a version of one story, with each angel book sharing common yet different threads. Each new piece of writing comes from a different vessel with different alignments. Every book is just another chapter in a much larger story. This book is no different. Your own personal experience with the angels is no different. Yet, when we put them all together, we create a mosaic of a much larger conversation, one that continues to bring new people into it each and every day. This is how collective consciousness works. We all play a part in weaving the story and charging the frequency.

For those of you who do have a religious practice, know that the angels will work with you in a way that aligns to your faith. Just don't expect them to behave the way your religion tells you they should, as you may be disappointed. For those of you who are a little like me and have shed the cloak of religion but are still faith- and belief-based, you will find yourself needing to readjust your mindset as well. The angels may test you the most, not because there is anything wrong with you but because you might be more reluctant and offer more points of resistance. For those of you who are not religious at all and are really wondering how on earth this book landed in your life, welcome! You are the perfect blank slate for the angels to start creating miracles in your life. For all of us, regardless of what group we find ourselves in, this work is a spiritual practice, and like all practices, it is deeply personal and our experiences will be our own.

Let's take a moment to talk about the "practice" part of spiritual practice, because this is the bit most people forget about. A practice is just that, something you practice each and every day. It is not one and done, and it is not like on a weekend retreat where someone hands you a pretty certificate. It is done every single day, or at least as often as possible so you build a habit and create momentum. I am not one who can preach about doing anything every single day, but more-often-than-not is still a practice. It is one of the reasons the ascension numbers work so well, because you will see them each and every day and will pay attention to them most days. Numbers are easy to be aware of. We see them on our clocks, our phones, our microwaves, and on license plates. Everywhere we go, there are numbers. Working with the angel ascension numbers is one of the easiest spiritual practices you can have. It is one of the reasons the angels have been pushing me to write this book for years, and it is the reason this book isn't just filled with affirmations and short snippets of number information, although there is nothing wrong with that approach, and I encourage it as a companion to this work.

This brings me to one last thing. As you make your way through this book, you may notice a bit of a theme, and that is my resistance in my work with the angels. I have always been reluctant, and I still am. You have no idea how lucky you are to be holding this book in your hands, as I have no idea when I will write another angel book. I am so resistant to this work, that I have never done any research into the angels themselves. They show up, they work with me for a bit, and then they shuffle off. It's quick, clean, and we have no emotional baggage. So, when I sat down to write this book, I started to doubt my knowledge and expertise around this topic. This resulted in me spending hours and hours on Google doing web search after web search about the angels in this book. I also bought about ten reference books on the topic as well. None of it was helpful to me, nor was it overly helpful for this book. However, it did at least let me know how others might come to the contents of this book. It let me see where you may have been before you landed here with me. In that respect, I guess it was more helpful than I first thought. Since I did not pull from any book or site directly, I do have one or two recommendations for you if you want a different perspective. One of the books I really liked was *Angel Prayers* by Kyle Gray. The other was *A Dictionary of Angels, Including the Fallen Angels* by Gustav Davidson. I have kept these two books in my library. I like them, and I think you will as well.

How This Book Works

Inside the chapters of this book you will find exercises, rituals, and journal work for you to do with each of the numbers and angels. For some of you, the terms and language won't be new, and you may already feel very comfortable using them and working your way through the exercises. If, however, this is the first time you have ever come across these words or you have never actively participated in these exercises before as a form of secular spiritual practice, I am going to walk you through what it all means in relation to this book. Either way, the angels and I have you covered, as we will now go over the five main concepts you will come across inside the chapters. They are altar work, prayer, healing, automatic writing, and chakras. While there is no wrong or right way to approach these ideas, concepts, or activities, the sections will give some insight into how you can approach the topics for the sake of this book if you feel the need to have a structured framework.

Altar Work

For some of you, the idea of setting up an altar may be a normal and natural thing for you to do. You may, in fact, already have one or several around your house. However, for those of you coming to the concept of an altar for the very first time, the whole idea may be confusing to you. An altar is a sacred space. It is somewhere you deliberately set as a place of spiritual devotion or for magical work. It can be a place to speak your prayers out loud and verbalize your needs and wants to the Universe. It could even be where you cast your spells or honor the changing of the seasons. I even have an altar for meditation. The point of the altar is to allow you to create a space where you can be focused and present with your spiritual self and your spiritual or magical work. Altars can be small or they can be large.

There are no rules about the size of an altar or even how you set one up. Some altars can be as simple as a vase of flowers, a candle, and a small figurine, angel, or some other deity. They can be placed on top of bookshelves, in the corner of a windowsill, or even set up next to your bed. Altars can also be quite large and elaborate, involving crystals, several candles, statues, money, feathers, pictures, wreaths, plants, and other found objects. Some of these items you may place deliberately on your altar: salt for protection, dirt to ground your wish, prayer, spell, or intention to the physical plane, or even a specific crystal to set an intentional energy. Other times you might just decorate it for beauty and aesthetics. You will notice in this book many different options on how you can set up altars for each of the individual angels. I highly suggest you create an angel altar somewhere in your home and change it out depending on which angel you are working with at any given time. Giving your altar a specific intention helps ground its power and keeps your energy focused and pure when you come before it to do your devotional work. This is why some people have more than one altar around their home and why I have several going at any given time. I know that when I come to my spell altar, I will be engaging in spellwork. I know that when I sit before my meditation altar, I will be meditating and nothing else. I know that when I light a candle on my goddess altar, I am deliberately choosing to invoke and work with the sacred feminine.

I think you get the idea, and it is an idea I want you to carry with you as you go about creating your angel altars. Make them personal. Make them intentional. This will help you with your angel work, and it will deepen your connection to the practice of angel ascension numbers. Each of the angels has an altar work section, so don't worry if this is the first time you have ever set up an angel altar. Also, while there are very detailed guidelines in each of the chapters about altars, feel free to be as playful as you want when setting your altar (or altars) up. They are meant to be deeply personal, and in many ways meant to become an extension of your sacred self. So have fun, trust your gut, and let the angels guide you on your altar work.

Prayer

Prayer is a form of communication between us and that which we call the Divine. It is when we seek council from that which we feel created us or is in a position to assist us. Prayer is an offering, a request, a call for help. Prayer is a form of spiritual magic and works the exact same way a spell does. It is the same energy, just different words. In this book you will often see the two phrases intermingled. This is so you can become as comfortable with the word "spell" as you are with the word "prayer" and vice versa. You will also notice throughout this book that the wording of each prayer or spell is more like an affirmation or a statement of thanks. In other words, the prayers and incantations are written in a way that presumes your request has already been answered. This is "thanking it forward," a trick the angels love to share with whoever is willing to listen. This makes prayer not something one does as a form of begging and pleading, but as a form of gratitude, release, and appreciation.

This is a very different type of prayer than what I was taught in church during my childhood, but then again, the type of praying I learned while on my knees, bent over on the hard wooden floors of the Catholic church, didn't really inspire me with much hope. Nor were these prayers filled with much in the way of joy. Most of the time they radiated fear. This is not the type of energy we want to be broadcasting out into the universe during our prayers or our spells. "Thanking it forward" is written all the way through this book. It is in the way the sentences have been constructed and the way the messages have been written in the connecting exercise in each of the chapters. The angels have really taken the guesswork out of it for you by providing you with thankful energy on each and every page. If, however, you want to move beyond this book and take this practice further, you can take the processes you have learned here and use them in other areas of your life. Thank yourself forward into healing. Thank yourself forward into abundance, joy, and fun.

Prayer work is a continuous thing. We never really stop and start it, as we are constantly putting ourselves in the hands of the Divine, and it is best to do it with a heart full of thanks. In each of the chapters, you will find prayers already written. Use them in their complete form or even use them to help you craft and mold something more personal. Just like everything else in this book, the prayers are there as a guide, a reference point, but they are not the be-all and end-all. Open your heart and feel into your prayer work, for the more deeply you connect with the thankful words of your prayers, the more power they will broadcast into the universe. Feel your prayers in your heart and welcome the angels into your life.

Healing

Throughout this book you will see the word "healing" used quite a bit. I feel it is important to discuss what this means in relation to this book and the angels themselves. First off, nothing in this book should take the place of real medical advice. Always consult a medical professional for a medical problem or a qualified mental health practitioner for therapy and trauma support. The healing work discussed in this book is something you would do in addition to the work you are already doing with your doctor or therapist. It is meant to support what you already have in play and to be an amplifier of the healing work you are already doing.

Healing as defined by the angels is allowing oneself to align to the frequency of unlimited and unconditional health and well-being. It is a vibrational experience that shifts your state of being, refocuses your mind, and supports your body's own instinctive healing abilities. This means that the angels and the ascension numbers are here to turbocharge and elevate the health team you already have in place. The angels do recommend you have a health and well-being team. Like all things in our physical work, collaboration in healing is a powerful tool. The more cheerleaders and champions you have in your health and well-being corner, the easier it is to stay in the flow of healing energy. In my private coaching practice I often have my clients find out who their healing angel is so they can add them to their healing team. What we find, as we move through our work together, is that adding this one extra element to the mix increases the client's receptivity to allowing healing into their lives. So, I guess you could say the healing work in this book is more about shifting your resistance to health and well-being, because the more you can drop your resistance to health, the more of it you can experience. The quicker you stop telling the old health story and start telling the new one, the easier it is for the work your doctor is doing to take effect.

The healing work you are doing throughout this book is opening you up to be more aware of the collaborative effects of your healing team. The more you increase your awareness around your specific place in the cocreated healing experience, the more healing energy can be received by your body, mind, and spirit. Every time you come across the word "healing" in this book, it is a reminder that your health and well-being team is here to support you and guide you in going both deeper and wider with your healing work. For some of you who work as healers, use the healing part of this book to work on yourself to refresh and restore your own healing energy because when you are at optimal health and well-being, then you are giving the best of yourself to your clients. Healing is an energy we are always in. It is constantly working with us, around us, and through us. No matter what is going on in our lives, we are experiencing healing energy. Stay open, follow the guidance of the angels, and allow them to keep you in the flow of healing energy.

Automatic Writing

Throughout the chapters of this book you are going to see automatic writing prompts, which is why I feel it is important to talk a little bit about what automatic writing means in the context of this book and your work with the angels and their numbers. Automatic writing is an intuitive practice. It is used to help people open up to Spirit and get them comfortable with receiving messages from nonphysical beings. It is such a fundamental process that I teach it to all my channeling students. In many respects, the majority of books you read are done through the process of automatic writing. In fictional work, the characters are channeled through the author, most times with prompts about what they desire. In nonfiction, we always start with questions or prompts about our content and then let the energy guide our research and writings. The automatic writing prompts in this book work much the same way. The angels can either be characters in your life story, or they can be part of your collective research. It is your choice.

The key to automatic writing is to let it flow unedited. Just let the words out on the page and worry about making sense of them later. For this book, you will be given a prompt inside the chapters. You will then sit with that prompt and write it out on a piece of paper. If you feel moved to do so, you can close your eyes, take a few deep breaths, and see the question being sent up to the angels. Next, you will pick up your pen and let the answer shoot through your crown chakra, down your arm, through your fingers, and out of your pen. Keep writing until you feel the energy or response is complete. Use what you have written for journal work if you find there is something that needs further investigation. If you read oracle or tarot cards, you may even feel the need to pull a card or two to follow up on what you have written down. This is all part of the automatic writing process.

Don't worry too much if at first you struggle to connect with a response or are unable to write more than a few words. This is all completely normal for beginners. Just stick with it. The more you work with the practice of automatic writing, the more words you will write, and the stronger your connection to the answer will be. There is no wrong or right way to do automatic writing. You dive in and see what happens. Lucky for you the angels are very good at this, and they will be patient and kind as you learn to talk with one another. Follow the prompts and allow them to lead the way.

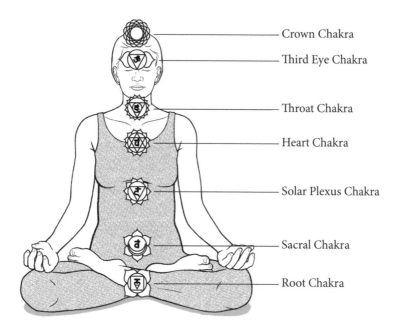

Crown Chakra

Third Eye Chakra

Throat Chakra

Heart Chakra

Solar Plexus Chakra

Sacral Chakra

Root Chakra

Chakras

Every so often you will see that I make reference to chakras or an individual chakra point throughout this book. For those of you who are completely new to these energy centers, let me give you a quick rundown of what I am talking about and why I have used them in relation to this book. Chakras, in their most simplified manner, are spinning disks of energy that move through the body. There are seven major chakras. They are as follows:

1. The root chakra
2. The sacral chakra
3. The solar plexus chakra
4. The heart chakra
5. The throat chakra

6. The third eye chakra

7. The crown chakra

These energy centers are considered vital to the function of our physical body and allow us to maintain optimal health and well-being. The root chakra, which starts at the bottom of your spine, draws the chakra energy up your body to the point of the crown. This allows energy to move up, through, down, and around your physical and energetic bodies. These energy centers have been used predominately in Eastern traditions for thousands of years as a form of healing, meditation, and self-actualization. Although chakra work has become a staple in many Western healing modalities, it is fairly new in Western culture and is still not as broadly spoken about outside New Age circles. The reason I include chakras in this book, even if it is on a very basic level, is because my work with the angels has been centered around energy healing. We have worked almost exclusively with the chakra system over the years, which means for me, chakras, angels, meditation, crystals, and numbers just all go together. That said, this is not a book about chakras. You won't find in-depth chakra information within these pages. If, however, you would like to explore this topic further and go even deeper into chakra work, then you are in luck, for I have a book dedicated just to chakras: *Tarot Healer: Using the Cards to Deepen Your Chakra Healing Work*.

Birth Angel Numbers

Throughout this book we will look at the angels and the numbers associated with them. You will work through connection exercises, rituals, and crystal magic. Up until now, I haven't really given you any strict guidelines about how, where, or when you may come across any of the numbers presented in this book. The most obvious place you may see these numbers would be clocks, which we have everywhere. Clocks are on your phone, in your car, on your microwave, on your walls, and if you wear a watch, on your wrist. I also mention license plates a couple of times throughout the book, but phone numbers and receipts for goods and services are just a few of the other examples where numbers can show up for you. We even had a car payment that was $333.33! In many respects these are numbers you randomly see or come across in your day-to-day life. You don't really have to dig too far or look too hard to notice these numbers, but there are other numbers you might want to explore, and they are the ones that connect you deeply to the angels. In this section, we are going to explore some of these numbers and find out who your birth angels are.

Now, for some of you this will be an easy process, as you will have their numbers jumping out at you the moment you write your date of birth. Some of you may have to dig a little deeper to find a match by looking over your entire birth numerology. These angels may show up in the time you were born, the date of your birth, or even the number of the hospital or location you were born in. Some of you may have two or three angels showing up in the date, time, and address of your birth location. If you are like me, you needed to be very closely watched this incarnation, so you ended up with more than one birth angel! Either way, there are a few ways to see which angels were hanging around waiting for you to jump back into physical form.

Uriel was in mine, as I have a very unusual amount of 5s in my numerology profile. The other angel who was hanging around was Raziel, as I have three 7s in my date of birth. I didn't realize this was such a big deal until I met a numerologist for the very first time in 2008 at a spiritual fair in Buffalo, New York. It was his fascination with my numbers that launched my own numerology obsession. From that point on, I could not look at any numbers without searching for patterns, codes, vibrational pathways, and of course, later on in my spiritual journey, angels. Who knows, maybe after reading this book, numbers will start to stalk you as well.

Let's start with the easiest place to find your birth angels, which is your date of birth. I have had clients who were born on the twelfth day of the twelfth month—12:12. Hello, Archangel Zeke! I have also done charts for people who were born on the eighteenth day of the eighth month 1968, which is 888. Hello, Archangel Raguel. As you write down your date of birth, do you have visible angel numbers? Don't worry if you can't see them right away, as you might have a date of birth like mine in which you have to go do some simple math to find them. My birthdate is the sixteenth day of the seventh month in 1972. Now, initially you can't see the three sevens. But as my Scottish numerology teacher showed me, 16 is really 7 hiding in plain sight. You see, numerologists don't focus on double digits, we look for single numbers, unless of course we are looking for a master or karmic debt numbers, which happen to be double digits, but that is not something we are looking for here. Now that we have found that third 7, we can see the 777 pretty clearly. So go over your birth date and see if you have some hidden numbers. You may even have to reduce your year of birth down to a single digit to find it. Go ahead and see what you come up with. You don't even have to have three, you might just have two that you can see. What I would recommend is to write those two numbers down, and then add up all the numbers of your date of birth and reduce them to a single digit. Add that digit to your repeat numbers and check which angel you have.

For example, let's say you were born on the second day of the second month in 1951. You would make it a math equation like this: $2+2+1+9+5+1 = 20 = 2+0 = 2$. Well look, now you have 222! Hello Jophiel! Let's do one more.

Let's say you were born on the twenty-sixth day of the sixth month in 1987, which would be $2+6+6+1+9+8+7 = 39 = 3+9 = 12 = 1+2 = 3$. Take your 3 and place it with your two 6s, and now you have 663. If you flip to Ariel's chapter, you will see this is one of Ariel's numbers, which means we just found your birth angel! Woohoo, yay us. As I said, sometimes you have to dig. Sometimes you really have to sit and let the numbers reveal the map. Eventually, you will get there.

Now, don't worry if you don't have any visible or hidden angels in your date of birth. Apparently only the ones we have to be constantly reminded about are out in plain sight. I mean, think about it, how often do you have to write your date of birth? You write it all the time. In fact, the older you get, the more you seem to have to write it. The angel in your date of birth wanted to be with you everywhere you went. It set the tone for every form, contract, or binding agreement to which you have ever had to add your date of birth. That's some serious angel blessing. However, not everyone needs to be that watched over.

Let's take a look at your time of birth if, of course, you know it. I don't know mine, which has always made astrology a headache for me, but if you do know it, see if you have any repeat numbers in it. Were you perhaps born at 11:11 a.m., or maybe even 2:22 p.m.? Some people will get lucky and see right away what numbers they have on their time of birth. Also, be on the lookout for other numbers in this book within the additional angel number sections in each chapter. Unlike your date of birth, you don't have too many numbers to play with here in regard to the time of your birth, so either the numbers are going to jump out at you or they are not. There is really nowhere to dig deeper here. However, if you were blessed to be born under an angel number, then this time of day is like a celestial portal for you. This is the time your connection with your angels is at its strongest. In other words, there was very little separation between you at the time of your birth—when the veil between the worlds was wide open—and both of you stood together, crossing dimensions and vibrational time, which makes the time of your birth powerful. If you do have an angel number for your time of birth, I would also use it as a portal for your manifestation energy. Set up an altar to this number and really channel it when you wish to create something meaningful in your life.

So, how is it going for you so far? Have you found your birth angel or angels yet?

Do not despair. We still have one set of numbers to go, and that is the address of where you were born. I know what you are thinking. I know you feel I'm really stretching it a bit here, but ask yourself, if the place of birth wasn't important, how come every astrologer everywhere wants to know it? Locale, darling. It's important. Where you were born holds a vortex of energy. It is the portal from which you sprang forth into the material world. It is where you crossed space and time to be here, during this time period, to join the rest of the planet. While I was writing this chapter, I thought I would look up the address of the hospital where I was born. It had two sets of repeating numbers: 77 and 55. In this example, 77 is the physical address, the 55 is part of its postal address. Good grief, okay, thank you angels. I think my two angels just felt they needed to hammer their presence home. So go and Google the address where you were born. Check it out. Maybe it will make you laugh out loud like mine did. Maybe it will shock the socks off you, or maybe, just maybe, it will answer so many questions you have had around the circumstances of your birth.

Righto, so what on earth do these numbers mean? Because this is an actual location, a fixed place, it is a center for that particular angelic energy. Mixed with your date and time of birth, it shows who and what energy the angel of place aligned for you at the beginning of this particular incarnation. That means that not everyone born at the location will have the same birth angels, because the angel of place mostly facilitated the alignments. However, like me, one of them may actually end up in your other numbers, and your angel of place may end up as your main birth angel, especially if this is the only angel number you have been able to identify so far. This would indicate a life lesson coming from your place of birth and a deeper connection to where you burst forth into the world of material things. It may also mean you have stayed living in the same location your whole life and the angel of place has blessed you with a sacred location. If this is you, congratulations! You are one of those people who never questions where home is, and you never feel compelled to find it. Honestly, I envy you.

If you want to take this even further and delve deeper into your numerology chart, I recommend the book *The Complete Idiot's Guide to Numerology*. It truly is one of the best numerology books I have ever come across for beginners. I recommend it to all of my students and have given away multiple copies of it over the years.

I hope this small introduction to discovering your birth angel has lit a fire in you about wanting to know more about your angel numbers and how they have played out, impacted, or set the tone in aspects or areas of your life. If, however, it was just a fun exercise and you never want to have to do that much math again, I totally get it. It can hurt your brain after a while. Just know that no matter which path you choose, the angels have always been with you and will stay with you long after you leave this mortal coil.

For now, though, continue on to the rest of this book. Walk the pages with the angels and start to learn about them, their numbers, and the teachings they have for you at this time. Each angel has something important to teach you, so just breathe, drop your shoulders, relax your neck, and stay open.

000 ~ ARCHANGEL METATRON
Spinning Infinite Possibilities into Your Life

"Everything is possible in this moment;
all you have to do is spin my cube and
see what portals of possibilities it opens."

Deeper Meaning of 000

The magic of 000 is that anything and everything is possible. Zero is the number of pure potential. Nothing has been decided upon, and everything is possible. It is only here in the vortex of the zeros that you can let your imagination run free. There is no failure and there is no success, only the hint of what can be. This means right now, in this moment, when 000 flashes before your eyes, the Universe is resetting your intentional vortex. It is giving you the option to start again. The angel number 000 is both nothing and everything all in one. It is empty and yet full. It is duality and wholeness. There is nothing the power of 000 cannot be, do, or have. It is freedom and yet contained creation. It is balance. Think of it as if you have three mysterious eggs. You have no idea what is in them until they finally crack open and reveal the prize inside.

While they stay sealed and whole, you can allow yourself to daydream about what could possibly be inside. It is this dreaming, this imagining, that Archangel Metatron wants you to tap into when you see these ascension numbers. As he comes to stand before you, he spins his cube by balancing one corner point on the tip of his finger as he spins it around like a basketball. It spins so fast that all you can see is an egg shape. There is no way of seeing the gaps or spaces between its metal frame as it spins, and that is the point. When creative potential is in motion, there are no gaps. The force of the energy fills in the space and creates an illusion of a solid shape. Your mind is much like this creative force; it fills in the gaps of your dreams and allows you to imagine them as complete and whole, and to see them from a space of having achieved them. Just like the eggs, the potential of what they could be is infinite.

So where do you want Metatron to focus his energy?

What spinning cube of creation do you want to infuse with the power of 000?

Take a moment to think about something that is playful, fun, and has been stalking your daydreams. Then let Archangel Metatron and 000 do the rest.

The Angel Metatron

If ever there was an angel who could teach us all about unlimited possibilities, it would be the one that started off just like us, as a human. Metatron's origin story is not like other angels—for unlike many of his vibrational angelic family, he has walked the physical plane as flesh and bone. He has awakened in more than one vibrational plane and is here to show us how we can do the same. We often wonder if angels walk among us, but the real question is, how can humans awaken from the limitations of the karmic world and walk amongst the angels? Transcending vibrational planes seems virtually impossible, but it can be done, and Metatron is the first example we have that it is possible. The biggest lesson from Metatron and 000 is not that anything is possible, though that is a fantastic lesson to learn, but that we are always going back to zero. There is no top; there is no end of the line. Instead we just keep landing back at zero. One of the biggest myths in the human realm right now is that once you have awakened things in your life, your world will get better. The truth, as Metatron explains it, is that awakening, or reaching alignment, is not the finish line, but rather it is merely the next point of resetting your vibrational frequency, and once you have obtained it, you go back to zero. Only at zero is everything possible.

Metatron teaches us that we see ascension as a game to up level, when really it is like a wheel. We take the ascension journey, and the wheel spins, bringing us back to zero. Though we are in the same place, we are now vibrating to a different frequency. He explains that we don't stop living the average human life after awakening, but instead, we just begin the vibrational game all over again. It is a game that will keep bringing us back to the same point over and over again. Only, each time we come back to zero, we view this point of return differently. We see different possibilities. We see different opportunities. In essence, zero becomes more until, eventually, zero becomes everything. This is what is being offered in the lesson of 000, which is that where you start, you also end, and where you end, you also begin. However, the you who returns is never the same.

Visualization/Meditation from Metatron: Opening to Your Unlimited Potential

In this guided meditation you will connect with Archangel Metatron and the vibrational energy of 000. There is no wrong or right way to experience this energy. It will show up differently for each of you. For some, you may feel sensations in your body, heat, cold, or even as if something or someone is touching your face and head as you move through the meditation script. For others, you might see colors, or your senses may become heightened. Some of you may feel nothing the first time you do this or maybe even the second or third time. It can take a moment to feel enough trust to really allow the energy into your experience. Just know that regardless of what does or does not happen to you, Metatron is there with you and will hold sacred space for you to explore all that will become visible to you. Make sure you do this meditation somewhere quiet and somewhere you will not be disturbed. If you feel called to, you can light a white candle. White candles are the go-to candle, as they hold and take on any energy or power we need them to. Have your candle burning throughout the meditation. Just remember to blow it out once you are done. You can record this script and listen to it so you can close your eyes, or you can simply keep your eyes open and read through the words. Either way, you will connect with energy and it will benefit you.

Do what is most comfortable for you.

Let us begin.

Go ahead and take a nice centering breath, breathing in through the nose and out through the mouth. As you breathe, relax the shoulders and feel your body settle into your seat. As you inhale, allow the breath to move gently into your heart center. On the exhale, release any and all resistance and tension that you were carrying before you sat down to do this meditation. Drop your shoulders, loosen your jaw, and allow your body to relax deeper and deeper with each slow, deep breath. Allowing your focus to move to your heart space, see a white light glowing where your heart is. Breathe gently in through the nose and out through the mouth. Keeping the focus on the white light at your heart center, watch as it expands out of your body and into the room.

Ask Archangel Metatron to step forward into this beam of white light. As he does so, think about something you want to create. It could be an opportunity, it could be a new income stream, it could be a new relationship, or it could be a new feeling of health and well-being. It doesn't matter what it is or how big or small the request may be, ask anyway. As Metatron steps through the light toward you, tell him what it is you desire and allow him to place it inside his cube. Watch as he takes your heart's desire, your request, and places it inside of his cube, while remembering to breathe in through the nose and out through the mouth.

Stand back as he begins to spin the cube, letting the energy of your heart's desire mix with the universal energy inside of his cube. As Metatron spins his cube, more possibilities and opportunities open within the vibrational vortex. More doors will open for you now, and more things will line up with ease and grace. Solutions will be easier to find, and the right people will show up at the right time. Take a nice deep breath in and wait for Metatron to walk back into the light beam of your heart. When he is done, he will simply turn and go, taking the cube and your heart's desire along with him. Trust that the Universe and Archangel Metatron are now conspiring for your greater good. Take another nice deep breath in and see the white light from your chest moving into all parts of your body now. As you inhale, see the white light pumping through you. As you exhale, see resistance and tension leaving your body. Allow the white light to wrap itself around you like a second skin. Once you are fully covered and contained in this energy, and with this white light wrapped around you, place your hand on your heart and say, "I open my heart to all that Metatron spins into my life." Now, take your hand away from your heart and just relax, breathing normally as you let the white light be absorbed into your skin. Allow yourself to become aware of and focused on your physical body and aware of and focused on the physical space you are in. Breathing nice and deep, become even more energized and aware as you bring your consciousness back to the here and the now, knowing that your heart's desire is in good hands, and all you have to do is be open to receive.

Setting Up an Altar to 000 and Archangel Metatron

This altar is for you to focus your energy when you know it is time to open yourself up to new opportunities and possibilities. You may even want to reset your vibes by intentionally working with 000. This can happen when you feel drained, lacking energy, or unmotivated or know you have come to the end of a cycle and have no idea how to proceed or what to do next. Bringing in the energy of 000 and Archangel Metatron will help hold the space between the gaps in your life, refill your cup, refresh your energy, and open yourself up to new beginnings. Metatron has grown in popularity over the last few years, so finding images and figurines of him is easier than it used to be. You may even have a Metatron oracle card that you can put on your altar. However you wish to honor him is entirely up to you. Just make sure you have something on your altar that represents him and his energy. Next, you will need a piece of paper with 000 and the intention or request you wish to have Metatron assist you with written on it. You can do this by hand, print it up, or do it in fancy calligraphy. It is entirely up to you. This is a personal space. You should decorate it in a way that "feels" right to you. Other things that you might want to put on your altar include flowers, crystals, salt, water, dirt, and of course, you will need a candle. Preferably you will include a white candle, as it is our all-inclusive candle. Make sure you set your altar up somewhere it will not be disturbed while you are actively using it. However long you decide to use your altar is entirely up to you. You may feel that you only need to do your prayer once, or you may feel called to do it for ten days. It really is up to you.

Once you have your altar set up, I recommend spraying it with a sage spray or giving it a once-over with sage or palo santo smoke. This will clear the space and set it up for your prayer work. When your altar is clean, set, and ready for you to start your prayer work, take a couple of nice deep breaths, light your candle, and speak your intention statement out loud, beginning with the words: "I call upon Archangel Metatron and the power of 000 to hear my intention and assist me in achieving it in the most magical way.

May this intention be for my higher good and the good of all those who may be involved." Then go ahead and read your intention statement/prayer: "My intention/prayer is…"

To end the ritual, you can either blow the candle out or leave it burning if it is safe to do so. If you choose to blow your candle out, repeat these words first: "As I blow this candle out, I trust that its smoke carries my intention up to the heavens to be manifested by the Universe. I am ready to receive my asking, and so it is." Next, blow out your candle. Your only job now is to stay open, observe, and write down any and all new ideas. Welcome any and all new friends, and keep yourself open. Remember, Metatron is spinning possibilities and opportunities into your life. The more observant you can become, the more you notice them. Know that what you have asked for is being created in your life and it is flowing to you right now.

Automatic Writing Prompts

After you have done your prayer work, or even after you have done the visualization, you will notice that your connection to Metatron will be open and messages and information will be starting to trickle or flow on through. If you feel moved to, pull out your journal and capitalize on this connection. Title your page "Talks with Metatron and the Vibrational Energy Known as 000." You can then just start writing, especially if you are used to journaling work. If you are not familiar with journal work, consider using these writing prompts to get you started and more familiar with the process:

1. Metatron, how will I know when you are around?

2. What area of my life does 000 want me to focus on and why?

3. How can I best allow new opportunities into my life?

4. What action step can I take today to move me closer to letting go of my fear and resistance to being open to new things?

5. How will aligning to the energy of 000 assist me today?

Angel Crystal: Clear Quartz

Clear crystal quartz is the "use all" crystal. It can be used in place of pretty much any stone. When in doubt, just grab your clear quartz. This is what makes it the perfect crystal to work with the 000 energy. It is full of potential, always open to possibilities; it loves newness and there is no wrong or right way to work with this powerful crystal.

For this exercise, you will need the magical tools of a quartz crystal pocket stone and a permanent marker. On your crystal you are going to write the number 000 as big as you can. Next, take your crystal and hold it in your nondominant hand, which is the hand you don't write with, as this is the receptive hand and the hand that is open to new energy. Wrap your fingers gently around your crystal, and hold it to your heart while you take a couple of nice grounding breaths. Feel the breath move all the way down your throat, through your body, and into the base of your spine. Once you feel present and focused, gently close your eyes and bring 000 to the forefront of your mind. Let it loom large in your mind's eye. As you keep your mind focused on the 000 in your mind's eye, invite Archangel Metatron into your energy. Ask him to fill your heart and your crystal with his energy and the energy of 000. You may see this energy flowing into your heart center as a light. It might have a color, or it might just be white. Do not try to control it; just let it flow.

Breathe slowly and deeply as you allow the energy in. Metatron will let you know when he is done by giving you a knowing nod of his head. Once he is done, allow the 000 to dissolve in your mind's eye. Release the connection to the visualization, and gently breathe yourself back into your body and back into the present moment. Remove your hand from your heart and place the crystal in your pocket, as it is now charged and ready to spin new possibilities into your life.

Additional Numbers for Working with Metatron's Energy

001—Let's begin again. A new beginning is happening, and it could be any area of your life. Do not resist it, do not try and control it, and just roll with it.

002—A new heart connection is waiting for you to acknowledge it. There could be a friend, coworker, or someone you have been talking to on social media who is ready to become more than a causal, infrequent acquaintance. This is not necessarily a romantic connection, but it could be just someone who has similar heart vibes as you.

003—Conversations with strangers will bring the most incredible insights. Answers come from the strangest places sometimes. Pay attention to new interactions today, as Metatron is broadcasting through everyone you meet.

004—Sometimes the little things you miss end up becoming the biggest things later on. Be mindful of the little things today.

005—Opportunities bring change. Possibilities require change. All things new bring changes that you may or may not have accounted for. When you see this number, know Archangel

Metatron is giving you a heads-up that new changes are on their way.

006—It might be a good time to come at an old relationship from a new perspective. All relationships need a refresh and an upgrade of energy. One of your current relationships is asking to be spun and refreshed.

007—New ideas spark new questions, which create new streams of learning. Keep your mind open today and see where a new thought takes you.

008—It's time to do something new with your body. Perhaps it is a haircut, new color, or how about some new clothes? Metatron is nudging you to start physically embodying all the new energy he is spinning into your life.

009—With all beginnings there are endings, and out of something old, something new is born. This is the transition of one cycle to another, and today you are smack in the middle of it. Lucky for you, Metatron is there, spinning you a path of potential.

111 ~ ARCHANGEL MICHAEL
Dare to Lead in a New Age

> "It is time to step up, drop your resistance,
> and move into a heart-centered leadership
> role in one or more areas of your life."

Deeper Meaning of 111

When Archangel Michael shows up, you can pretty much guarantee things are about to get a makeover. Right now, there is an area of your life that needs you to step into and claim it. Only your energy will do, so no more delegating in this area of your life. The angel number 111 isn't about any old leadership—no, here in the energy of ascension, this is all about heart-based leading. Learning to trust you heart and using it to teach others how to trust their hearts is the leadership of the new age. This new leadership that Archangel Michael invites into your life with the power of 111 flows with the vibration of love. In fact, one cannot stand on the leading edge of Source energy without having an open heart. Michael wields the sword of truth, as it cuts through fear, doubt, guilt, shame, sadness, disconnection, and anger. When these energies no longer block your life, true heart energy can flow. You are being asked to look at an area of your life that needs this sort of leadership. Is it your finances, your relationships, your health, or your career? Maybe you can identify more than one area, but one of them needs you right now more than the others. It needs you to pick up Michael's sword and rid yourself of any threads you have to non-loving energy. Cut all that binds you and stand victorious. Claim your peace of mind. Claim your power. Claim your space in the spotlight of your heart, for to lead is to be vulnerable. The angel number 111 reminds us that there is no leadership without the courage to be vulnerable. You have to be seen, you have to be heard, and most of all you have to feel worthy of all of those things. When 111 flashes into your experience, you can be sure that Archangel Michael is offering you his sword. However, in order for you to be able to wield it, you are going to need the strength to open your heart.

The Angel Michael

Archangel Michael is a natural-born leader. He has spent his entire existence on the battlefield of love. Each and every day you will find him slaying all things that stand in the way of bringing a loving world to all who desire it. Of all the angels, Michael is the one who is pushing the hardest for an ascended and awakened humanity. It is his goal to get every sentient being to the next level of expansion and enlightenment. You could say this was why Michael was created: to assist us on the path of love and to get us to stand up and claim our place in the kingdom of light, which will be the next phase for all sentient begins. Michael is a tireless crusader who doesn't know what it means to give up or give in, but he does know when to stop, pause, or even step aside. He leads by example, always, which is why he is not out there trying to convince others to be on his team. Michael is no salesman. Instead, he just shows up and is himself.

Michael's mission is not to get followers, although he gains them everywhere he goes. His very existence is his mission, and that is what he teaches us. We are the mission. We are the leaders of our own lives and, through this act, we lead others. The essence of 111 is to be ourselves always and without apology. We limit ourselves when we feel we aren't living up to someone else's version of who we are. The truth is, that is not why we came to play in these physical bodies, and Michael knows this. He understands, which is why he stands before you now, and every time you see 111, he offers you his hand. He wants you to walk out of the shadows of limitation and into the light of your divine potential. Lead your life your way, on your own terms, and with a love for yourself bigger than the love you ever expected from someone else.

Visualization/Meditation from Michael:
Step Up and Claim Your Spot on the Leaderboard

In this guided meditation, you will be able to connect with the leadership energy of Archangel Michael. There is no wrong or right way to experience this energy. It will show up differently for each of you. For some, you may feel sensations in your body, heat, cold, or even as if something or someone is touching your face and head as you move through the meditation script. For others, you might see colors, or your senses may become heightened, and some of you may feel nothing the first time you do this or maybe even the second or third time. That is fine, and it is completely normal. Just know that regardless of what does or does not happen to you, Michael is there with you, protecting you and holding space for you to explore the areas in your life where you need to take the lead. Make sure you do this meditation somewhere quiet where you will not be disturbed. If you feel called to, you can light a golden candle and have it burning throughout the meditation. Just remember to blow it out once you are done. You can record this script and listen to it so you can close your eyes, or you can simply keep your eyes open and read through the words. Either way, you will connect with energy and it will benefit you.

Do what is most comfortable for you.

Let us begin.

Start by finding a nice comfortable chair to sit in, one in which you can sit with your feet on the ground, your back relatively straight, and your arms comfortably by your side. Take a couple of nice centering breaths and relax into your seat, keeping your eyes open if you wish, or if you have recorded this meditation, close your eyes ever so gently. As you sink deep into the breath work, focus on an aspect of your life where you feel either overwhelmed or powerless, or even an area of your life that doesn't particularly excite you. Bring this to the forefront of your mind, making sure it is in brilliant, vibrant color so that you can see it clearly. Make sure it is in clear focus and that there is no way you could possibly mistake this for anything else. Just observe the picture or scene that is playing out in front of your mind's eye. There is no space for judgment here. Just allow the feelings that you have to flow through you as you observe this area or aspect of your life. Don't judge these feelings; just allow them to bubble up.

Now, be honest: How would you like to resolve these feelings? What would make you feel empowered, in control, more connected to this area of your life that you have not yet taken the lead in?

The reason that you have neglected these aspects or areas of your existence is because there is a piece of you that doesn't feel that you are capable of handling them. This is when we call in Archangel Michael and ask him to guide you, support you, and lead the way in these aspects of your life. See him standing beside you, ready to help. Watch as he rolls up his sleeves and gets ready for work. Listen carefully as he gives you instructions on how to take the first step in connecting to these areas and aspects of your life.

Do not judge the simplicity or complexity of what he is telling you; just listen and observe. Allow him to guide you back to the path of confidence and restore your faith in your own abilities to lead the life you truly desire. If any emotions come up that feel difficult or challenging, merely ask Archangel Michael to handle them for you. It is, after all, his specialty. Once Michael has given you instructions and guided you on your first steps, just take a deep breath. As you breathe, bring the image of your life that you started with at the beginning of the meditation back to the forefront of your mind and see if it has changed.

Does it look and feel different than it did before?

What emotions now flow through you as you observe this picture or scene?

Don't get into analysis; simply allow your feelings to rise and fall. When you have seen enough, allow the image to dissolve, knowing that you and Archangel Michael now have this under control. It may not be perfect, and it may still take some time to even feel comfortable, but it is being steered in the right direction. Take a nice deep breath and relax your body as you thank Michael for coming and being with you today. Once he has gone, relax your breathing and bring your focus and awareness back to your body and back to the room around you. Notice that with each breath you ground deeper and deeper back into your body and your mind, which should be laser sharp, alert, and ready for any and all inspired leadership action.

Setting Up an Altar to 111 and Archangel Michael

Of all the angels, Michael is the most dominant in our current timeline. Many people already have altars to Michael, as statues and candles are readily available with his energy already in them. Archangel Uriel calls Michael the pinup boy of the new age, which is funny, but true. If, however, you do not have any Michael-inspired items in your home, that is perfectly fine, and you don't really need them. You can use any candle, though he really likes gold, as it is regal and luxurious. You can also use any image of Michael you like for your altar. It could be an oracle card, a Google image search printout, a painting, whatever you are drawn to. The most important part of this altar is to have something that represents Michael on it, a candle, and a piece of paper with 111 written on it. How you choose to decorate your homage to Michael is entirely up to you. Just make sure you have this particular altar set to match the vibration of the energy you are calling in, including leadership, specifically heart-centered leadership. Next, write your intentional prayer statement. This is something you will write related to the sort of leadership you know you need to step into.

An example might be something like: "My intention is to step up in my relationship and take charge of all the tasks my partner really struggles with. I claim my place in the relationship and understand I am responsible for the energy I put into it. I intend to allow Michael to stand beside me, to guide me and to direct me."

Once you have your altar set up, I recommend spraying it with a cleansing spray or waving the smoke from an herb wand over it. This will cleanse and clear the space and set it up for your prayer work. Next, take a couple of nice deep breaths, light your candle, and just focus on the golden light of the flame. See this golden energy growing bigger and encompassing your altar and even yourself. Now, go ahead and speak your intention statement out loud, beginning with the words: "I call on Archangel Michael and the power of 111 to hear my intention and assist me in achieving it in the most miraculous way. May this intention be for my highest good and the good of all those who may be involved." Then go ahead and read your intention statement/ prayer: "My intention/prayer is…" Make sure you are using a commanding voice and confident tone, as you are tapping into the energy of divine leadership.

To end the ritual, you can either blow the candle out or leave it burning if it is safe to do so. If you choose to blow your candle out, repeat these words first: "As I blow this candle out, I trust that its smoke carries my intention up to the heavens to be manifested by the Universe. I am ready to receive what I am asking for, and so it is." Next, blow out your candle.

Your job is now to step up and claim the spaces in your life that you need to lead in, knowing that Michael is walking beside you, supporting you, and infusing you with the courage to keep moving forward.

Automatic Writing Prompts

After you have done your prayer work, or even after you have done the visualization, you may notice that your connection to Michael is open and messages and information will be starting to trickle or flow on through. If you feel moved to, think about pulling out your journal and capitalizing on this connection. Title your page "Talks with Michael and the Vibrational Energy Known as 111." You can then just start writing if you are somewhat used to journaling work. If you are not, consider using these writing prompts to get you started and more familiar with the process:

1. Michael, how will I know when you are around?
2. What area of my life does 111 want me to focus on and why?
3. Why have I been scared in the past to step up and claim my place in certain areas of my life?
4. What action step can I take today to move me closer to letting go of my fear and resistance?
5. How will stepping into the energy of 111 assist me today?

Angel Crystal ~Tiger's-Eye

Tiger's-eye helps bring the vibrational, emotional, mental, and physical body into alignment so it can act with discernment. It promotes focused and strategic action, just like Michael and the power of 111. This is the stone you need when you need to step up in an area of your life. Armed with the energy of tiger's-eye, the vibration of 111, and the power of Archangel Michael, you will step confidently into heart-centered leadership.

For this exercise, hold your crystal in your dominant hand, which is the hand you write with. Wrap your fingers around it, but don't squeeze it too tightly. Take a couple of nice deep breaths and, if you feel called to, you might even slowly close your eyes. As you hold the crystal and allow your breath work to become rhythmic, bring to mind a time in your life when you felt brave, such as a time when your confidence was higher than normal and you did something that made you feel strong, in control, and empowered. It doesn't have to be a big thing. We are just searching for a moment that connects you to a feeling. Take a snapshot of this moment in your mind's eye and allow the feelings to move down your arm and into the crystal in your hand. As you do this, you may feel your hand start to tingle, get warm, or even get cold. This is all normal. Just maintain your breath work and move the emotions and feelings down into your crystal.

When you feel you are complete, I want you to open your hand and ask Archangel Michael to infuse your crystal, this wonderful piece of tiger's-eye, with his energy and the power of 111. You may feel sensations on or across your skin, like a small breath or like feathers brushing across your hand, or you may feel nothing at all. This is all normal. Just maintain the breath work. When you feel Michael is finished or you just get that knowing sensation, close your hand once again, bring the crystal up to your heart, and just allow the energy of the crystal to merge with your heart center. Take slow, deep, relaxed breaths. When you feel more confident, more at peace, or just have a sense of relief, you can take your hand away from your heart, and if you had your eyes closed, open them. Your tiger's-eye crystal is now infused. Keep it in your pocket, on your altar, or in your bag or purse. Use it as a talisman when you need a boost of strength and courage.

Additional Numbers for Working with Michael's Energy

112—One of your relationships needs you to step up and lead. No more sitting back waiting for the other person to solve this particular problem. You are the solution, so claim it.

113—It's time to organize a social get-together. Host a movie night, dinner party, night at the theater, or weekend away. Be the one who brings your friends together to honor their place in your life.

114—One of the great strengths of any leader is their ability to create a well-organized system or structure that keeps them organized and in the flow. Now is the time to create one that works for you.

115—Leaders can change with the wind. They are fluid, flexible, and understand that all things move and shift. You are being reminded to bend with the breeze so you don't snap in any oncoming storms.

116—We teach others how to care for themselves by showing them how we care for ourselves. Show the example you want others to adopt as you make personal care a priority.

117—Knowledge is power and wisdom is strength. Keep your mind sharp, deep, and always open to new ideas.

118—Learning to master your senses allows you to navigate the physical world around you. Be mindful of what the five senses tell you, but don't let them limit your potential.

119—Leaders are always thinking about what sort of lasting legacy they will leave behind, something that will continue long after they have dropped their physical vessel. You are being prompted to consider what you are leaving behind. Michael asks, "How will you be remembered?"

222 ~ ARCHANGEL JOPHIEL
Bring in Twin Flame Energy

"You are being wrapped in the wings of
Archangel Jophiel as she infuses you
with healing twin flame energy."

Deeper Meaning of 222

At this moment one of your twin flames is thinking about you. It doesn't matter which one; it could be any one of your multiple twin flames. What is important in this moment is that together you are creating a vortex of energy based on how you are currently feeling. Right now, you are both sharing a thought, a feeling, a memory, a slice of time and space that only the two of you can access. Place your hand on your heart and take a breath. Slowly relax and feel the energy moving through your chest as you inhale and exhale. Allow the breath to calm you, support you, and remind you that you do not walk this experience alone. The angel number 222 is a reminder that you share a vibrational connection to another. If you notice that the moment you saw 222 you were not feeling particularly happy or in a good headspace, know that your twin flame is also open to sharing your pain and sadness. The angel number 222 lets you know that you are not obligated to carry your burdens by yourself—that there is another out there that is more than happy to help you. They will breathe with you and slowly but surely move you into a better-feeling place. The angel number 222 is a reminder that you are loved and supported no matter how you are feeling or what you are thinking. When we see 222, we also know that Archangel Jophiel is with us, showing us the beauty of our experience and nudging us to allow more love into our lives. It is often easier for us to give love than it is to receive, which is another reason you are seeing 222. Your twin flame doesn't just take—they give, effortless like breathing. You cannot just exhale and never inhale. When you see 222 it is an indicator that you are in the flow of giving and receiving even if you are not aware of it. That your twin flame is connecting to you across space and time to share in an exchange of energy.

The Angel Jophiel

Archangel Jophiel is the angel of beauty and creation. She has a twin flame connection to Archangel Metatron, and together they have a lot to teach us about twin flame energy. I have learned a lot from Jophiel regarding what this energy means and what it doesn't. For one, this energy is not romantic. It is connective energy, and it is one that has a deep love that runs through it—a love that far surpasses anything we could limit, control, or label. This makes it such healing energy to work with. It is through working with Jophiel that I have learned to open myself up to so many types of loving relationships. She has shown me how twin flame energy works and why it is so important to invite it into our lives.

Here in the sacred space that 222 holds for you, you can take a moment to stop whatever you are doing, place your hand on your heart, take in a nice deep breath, and think of someone important to you and for whom you have a deep love. Visualize them smiling and happy and hold that image. Next, send that pure, complete, deep, and true nonjudgmental love their way. You only need to do this for a few breaths, as in that moment, you have swept them with Jophiel's beautiful, healing, twin flame energy. It is important to understand that twin flames are not halves of anything. Their purpose is not to complete us or fill any perceived gaps in our lives. Quite the opposite, our twin flames are enhancers: they help us sustain our spark by seeing us as complete and whole and with an unconditional love that only a twin flame can have. There is nothing you can do, have, be, or say that will ever diminish your worth, purpose, or reason for being in your twin flame's eyes.

Twin flame energy and the power of 222 let you know that you are in sync with one of your twin flames. You think and feel similar things at similar times to one another. You have a spooky connection to another, in which things about your lives echo in terms of experience. It's almost like you were separated at birth but in another dimension, and now somehow you have converged here on this plane, together at the same time, to keep each other's hearts wide open. Although we have many twin flames in the physical realm, we also have twin flames in non-physical form, which means it doesn't matter which twin flame you connect with when 222 comes into your experience. Jophiel wants you to think of it this way: Imagine yourself in a room of mirrors and everywhere you look, you see yourself. You do not just see half of you but all of you, for you are not half a person or half an energy. However, you also know it's not you, even though it may look like you. There is a feeling of familiarity, but there is a difference at the same time. This, she says, is what a twin flame feels like. It is similar but different, in form and out of form, as it makes no difference because it is never about the person, but rather it is always about the feeling, the vibe, and the connection.

This is why you can connect with twin flames even if you know one of your twin flames has either long since dropped their physical costume or has never walked a physical incarnation. Right now, just reading this chapter, you are connecting to the twin flame energy of the angels. From the moment you picked up this book and started to read it, you allowed yourself to be flooded with angelic twin flame energy. All you had to do was decide to flip the pages of this book, which was more of a feeling than a thought—you could even say it was a flash of inspiration, much like the power of 222.

Visualization/Meditation from Jophiel: Opening to the Healing Power of Twin Flame Energy

In this guided meditation, you will be able to connect with angelic twin flame healing energy. There is no wrong or right way to experience this energy. It will show up differently for each of you. For some, you may feel sensations in your body, heat, cold, or even as if something or someone is touching your face and head as you move through the meditation script. For others, you might see colors, or your senses may become heightened. Some of you may feel nothing the first time you do this or maybe even the second or third time. Just know that regardless of what does or does not happen to you, Jophiel is there with you. She is cradling you in her wings and pumping the healing force of twin flame energy into your vibrational body.

Make sure you do this meditation somewhere quiet where you will not be disturbed. If you feel called to, you can light two pink candles and have them burning throughout the meditation. Just remember to blow them out once you are done. You can record this script and listen to it so you can close your eyes, or you can simply keep your eyes open and read through the words. Either way, you will connect with energy and it will benefit you.

Do what is most comfortable for you.

Let us begin.

Take a nice deep breath in through the nose and out through the mouth, and another, again in through the nose and out through the mouth. Extend the breath, drawing it deeper into the lungs. As you feel your chest expand, relax the shoulders and feel the tension start to slowly release from your neck and back, feeling this wave of relaxation moving down your spine and relaxing the tailbone, hips, legs, knees, ankles, and toes. As you take another nice deep breath in through the nose, exhale any resistance out through the mouth.

Dropping into a deeper state of relaxation, focus this breath work through the heart center, breathing in through the nose and out through the heart, slowly but surely expanding the heart center. If you feel any discomfort, slow the breath work down and breathe deeper not faster. As the heart center expands, focus on the light that is emanating from your heart chakra. With each exhale, see this light extending out further and further. Take a nice, deep, slow breath, letting the light expand until it surrounds your body, holding you in a beautiful protective bubble.

Ask now for Archangel Jophiel to come into your awareness as she holds this protective bubble gently in her arms, cradling you and your heart energy. As her hands make contact with this beautiful, protective bubble, she infuses it with twin flame healing power. This may change the color of your protective bubble, or it may keep it the same. It may make it glitter and sparkle and shine. Every time you inhale, you breathe this energy in. With each slow, deep breath, this beautiful twin flame healing energy moves into your body. Feel it as you breathe in, the energy hitting the back of your throat, traveling down to your lungs, expanding the chest cavity, and moving down into the stomach and lower abdomen. Feel this energy as it moves into the hips, down your legs into your feet and your toes.

Take another nice deep breath of this twin flame healing energy, and feel it move down your arms, over your elbows, and into your wrists and fingers. Feel this energy, this healing Source energy Archangel Jophiel is pumping into you, move down your spine, your shoulders, and your back, into the base of your spine, and across your buttocks. Taking another nice deep breath, feel this healing energy move up into your mouth, your teeth, your tongue, your gums, across your cheeks, into your ears, through your sinuses, your eyes, up into your third-eye point, and out the top of your head.

Hold your hands out with your palms facing up so that this energy can radiate through you. Not being blocked, this flow of energy moves through the soles of your feet, the palms of your hands, and out the top of your head. Breathing deep now, allow this energy into every cell in your body. Breathe the energy in through your nose, exhaling any resistance you may have in accepting it into your being. Allow this twin flame energy to infuse you with love, support, guidance, and a sense of belonging. Breathing even deeper now, sinking further and further into the arms of Jophiel, feel yourself floating as she cradles you and offers this healing just for you. Just breathe, relax, and allow.

If there is anything you wish to surrender or give to the angel, now is the time to release it. Send it out through your heart and into the protective bubble. Watch as it floats up into Jophiel's hands. Allow her to remove it out of your aura—which is the field of energy that surrounds your body—once and for all. Taking another deep breath, let go and relax. Next, ask Jophiel to finish up her healing work and to finish clearing any spaces in the auric field, which may be blocked to your twin flame energy. Also, ask her to remove anything out of the arch line—the space in your auric field that runs from one shoulder over your head to the other shoulder—that no longer serves you. Once she is finished, thank her for showing up today and offering you this angelic healing.

Take a nice deep breath now, and with each inhale, bring your energy back into your body, breathing it all in with slow, steady, deep breaths. With each breath, you're becoming more and more aware of your physical body. You're becoming more grounded, alert, and attentive. Take another deep breath and bring your awareness back to this space and time and to this moment, becoming more focused. After one last slow, steady breath, open your eyes, wiggle your toes, and roll out your shoulders.

Setting Up an Altar to 222 and Archangel Jophiel

Out of all the angels, Jophiel is the girliest girl of them all. It is not very often I like to double down on gendering vibrational energy, but this is Jophiel and she has no problem being the pink, sparkly girl of the angelic realm. That said, if she does not present this way to you, that is perfectly fine. She does present this way to me and has done so for most of the people I have worked with over the years. Keep in mind that not all the angels will align with how I have presented them in this book, and Jophiel is no exception. However, do not be surprised as you set up your altar to her and the energy of 222 if lots and lots of pink ends up on it. This is her way of opening your heart and slowly, subtly, bringing heart chakra vibes into your life and infusing your energy with it. It has been through Jophiel that I have learned the true healing power of the color pink, and trust me, never in a million years would I have ever thought I would own anything pink. Now there are flashes of pink everywhere in my house, on my altars, and in my wardrobe. Working with twin flame energy is about embodying the energy. Jophiel does this through her color choices, which are primarily all shades of pink. The things you will need for your twin flame altar include a picture of Jophiel, a pink candle, 222 written on a pink piece of paper, some salt, a pinch of dirt, some feathers, and as many sparkly things as you can personally stand. You will also want to sit down and compose a prayer or intention statement to Jophiel and 222. For example, it might say, "Jophiel, I allow you to align me to my twin flame energy. I allow you to slowly and lovingly open my heart and shower me with twin flame love."

Once you have your altar set up, I recommend spraying it with a clearing spray or giving it a once-over with the smoke of an herb wand of your choice. This will assist in mentally, physically, and spiritually clearing the space and setting it up for your prayer work.

Once your altar is prepped and ready, take a couple of deep breaths, light your candle, and speak your intention statement out loud, beginning with the words: "I call on Archangel Jophiel and the power of 222 to hear my intention and assist me in achieving it in the most loving way. May this intention be for my higher good, as well as the good of all those who may be involved in this intention coming to pass." Then, go ahead and read your intention statement/prayer: "My intention/prayer is..."

To end the ritual, you can blow your candle out or leave it burning if it is safe to do so. If you choose to blow your candle out, repeat these words first: "As I blow this candle out, I trust that its smoke carries my intention up to the heavens to be manifested by the Universe. I am ready to receive what I have asked for, and so it is." Then, blow out your candle.

Now that you have cast your spell/prayer, your job is to stay open and alert. I know this seems silly, but you will start to notice more and more pink and that, along with the number 222, will let you know you are healing your heart, opening your twin flame connection, and aligning yourself to deeper love.

Automatic Writing Prompts

After you have done your prayer work, or even after you have done the visualization, you will notice that your connection to Jophiel may be more open and messages and information may start to trickle in or flow into your awareness. If you feel moved to do so, think about pulling out your journal and capitalizing on this connection. Title your page "Talks with Jophiel and the Vibrational Energy Known as 222." Because this is Jophiel, you might find yourself highly attracted to glitter pens, and if this is the case, just roll with it. If you have worked with Jophiel in the past, you might be ready to launch into some journal work with her and just see what twin flame messages she has for you, or you may consider using these writing prompts to get you started and more aligned with Jophiel's energy:

1. Jophiel, how will I know when you are around?
2. Which of my twin flames does 222 want me to focus on and why?
3. Why have I struggled in the past to form a healthy relationship with my twin flame energy?
4. What action or step can I take today to move me closer to letting go of my fear and resistance?
5. How will stepping into the energy of 222 assist me today?

Angel Crystal: Ametrine

This crystal infuses the vibration of two different stones—amethyst and citrine—and merges them into one. It holds the perfect vibration of two beings sharing an experience. This is why ametrine brings the vibration of 222 and the energy of Archangel Jophiel together in one.

Magical materials you will need for this exercise include an ametrine pocket stone, two single dollar notes or coins, a piece of paper (a sticky note will do just fine), and a pink marker or gel ink pen. On your paper, write the number 222 as big as you can, filling the paper. Once done, place it where you can see it. Next, take your ametrine and your two single dollars. If you have dollar notes, wrap the crystal in the money. If, however, you have coins, just hold them along with your crystal in your non-dominant hand, which is the hand you don't write with. Place your pocket stone and your money over your heart, and gaze at the number 222 written in big pink writing. Steady yourself and deepen your breathing, then repeat this short prayer:

> *Dear Jophiel,*
>   *Come to me. Bless me with your energy and show me how to open my heart to my twin flames. Infuse this crystal with the power of 222 so I can keep your blessed vibration near me at all times. Connect my money with that of my twin flames so I know that when I carry these notes or coins around with me, I am doubling my blessings. Open my eyes to the beauty in my life and guide me to my next twin flame connection. Divine angel, I honor you, and I am in service to you. Thank you for being here with me now. As it is above, so it is below.*

Dispose of your paper and carry your crystal around with you when you need to feel the connection to the power of 222 or want to call in Jophiel's twin flame power. Place your notes or coins into your purse, handbag, or wallet, and carry them around with you for approximately seven days. Then spend them, releasing the energy of the twin flame blessings into the world. You can repeat this exercise anytime you want to be reminded of how blessed you are or when you want to add more twin flame blessings into the world of commerce.

Want to supercharge your twin flame crystal? Of course you do! To do this, put your ametrine crystal in the windowsill when you go to bed and leave it there until lunchtime the next day. This simple step will make sure your crystal is supercharged with both lunar and solar energy.

Additional Numbers for Working with Jophiel's Energy

220—One of your twin flames is aligning you with a new heart-centered opportunity.

221—One of your twin flames is urging you to take on more of a mentoring role with someone in your community or workplace. Just stay open.

223—It's twin flame manifesting time. Your manifesting energy is double the power, so be mindful of your thoughts, since what your mind repeats it will create twice.

224—One of your twin flames wants you to stop what you are doing and count four blessings right now. Say them out loud so you can capture the energy of the moment.

225—One of your twin flames is creating a positive change in your life, so look for things that go right today, as they are signs that even more positive flow is coming your way.

226—Stop what you are doing, place your hand on your heart, and just say, "I love you."

227—An opportunity to learn something new is being lined up by one of your twin flames. This new path of wisdom could come from anywhere, so be on the lookout.

228—Tell your body you love it and that you love its ability to connect to your twin flames. Take a breath and really feel it move in and out of your body.

229—A karmic cycle with one of your twin flames is coming to an end. Be on the lookout for endings, and don't try to stop the closing down of its energy.

333 ~ ARCHANGEL HANIEL
Let Your Heart Be the Music for Your Ears

"The language of the heart is much more
playful than most of the words you
hear with your ears. Listen to the beats,
groove with the rhythm, and dance
your way to better-feeling vibes."

Deeper Meaning of 333

The angel number 333 is a reminder that your ears, what you are hearing, and the sounds around you need to be in alignment with the language of your heart. The heart has a playful and joyous tune, one that flows in a natural and steady rhythm. It thrives on positive, upbeat, "can-do-it" language. The heart knows no limits and doesn't understand the language of lack, fear, doubt, guilt, or shame, so much so that the heart will automatically contract when these words are being vibrated into being via your voice. The angel number 333 is the push you need to get back into a more loving and compassionate dialogue with yourself and those around you.

Archangel Haniel wants to connect you back to your joy, your well-being, and above all, your deep, true, unconditional love for life. Many of us have moments when we love our lives. We have moments that we wish would last forever and moments that we consider too good to be true. Archangel Haniel wants you to know there is no "too good to be true," and if you are constantly seeing 333, she wants you to reach for those moments, the ones you thought you were only entitled to every so often. She wants you to keep them close to your heart, have them polarized in your mind, and use them to become the language your heart learns to seek out. She wants you to understand that these "to-good-to-be-true" moments are the true moments of your divine self. There is no limit to them, as limit is a belief and a construct of the mind. The heart, however, knows no limit. The angel number 333 is the reminder that joy is not something only given to those who deserve it or to those who feel it's their turn. It is an unlimited state that you can tap into whenever and wherever you want it. It's yours, so take it.

Archangel Haniel says it all starts with what you listen to. What is in your ears? What are the words you listen to and the things you say? The vibrational vortex of the language around you sets the tone of everything you experience. Haniel and 333 say, "Listen, really listen, and pay attention. What tune does your life have? What song do you have on repeat, and are you truly paying attention to how it is creating the world you engage in?" It is funny, in an ironic kind of way, that we as humans need these sorts of things pointed out to us. Oftentimes they need to be pointed out repeatedly because just like repeating numbers, we need to see things often before we really notice them. When 333 flashes into your life, just know it is time to find things that bring a smile to your face and a swing to your hips. Be sure you take every opportunity of joy that crosses your path. Tune in to the radio of your heart and let it be your guide. Find the channel that lights you up, pumps your soul, and moves you into the flow of the unlimited divine happiness that is yours for the taking.

The Angel Haniel

Archangel Haniel is connected to the planet Venus, the great goddess of love, beauty, pleasure and, of course, joy. In many respects Haniel is the archangel that helps us connect to what it means to embody divine love and divine joy. This means being able to connect these intangible concepts to something tangible, such as your physical body, which is why she likes to be connected to music. Nothing quite gets you connected to your body the way music does. Music moves you. It has the ability to fill you up, transform your mood, increase your radiance, and alter your emotional state. When we think about Haniel's connection to the goddess of love, it makes sense she would want us to be so careful about how we are nourishing ourselves. Like all good mothers, she only wants us to have the best, which is why she likes to send you those 333 reminders. They are basically big shoutouts saying, "How are you nourishing your mind, heart, and soul today, dear one?"

Words have power, and no one knows this more than Haniel. She also knows your mind will go along with whatever you tell it, so tell it good things. Tell it beautiful things. Tell it things you would tell someone you truly and deeply love. This is a fantastic way to think about what we allow ourselves to listen to. For example, would you want someone you love to only be listening to language that constantly pulled them down and diminished them? Of course you wouldn't. If you saw someone you love beating themselves up over and over again, you would do everything in your power to make them stop. Well, think of Haniel and 333 as your reminder to stop beating yourself up. She wants you to instead find something good to plug into your ears, something that will make you come alive, bring you peace, and allow you to flow with the divine beat of the Universe's love drum. Haniel wants to know what is in your heart. She is very interested in what it has to say. She wants to learn how it beats and what sort of things make it feel alive.

Archangel Haniel knows how often we humans talk ourselves out of beautiful, loving experiences. We question ourselves and any other people involved and start to doubt our need for things that we have been taught are frivolous or unnecessary, even though the heart desires them and aligns to their language. Haniel's lessons can be tricky, and I know they have been for me. I, for one, had been very programmed to only look at socially acceptable life essentials. I have learned through her that what the heart deems essential is not going to be what someone else's heart deems essential. In other words, what makes your heart sing is not going to make someone else's heart sing because we all desire different things. This is really the lesson of 333, which is that having what you want through listening to your heart just opens the door for others to also listen to their heart and have what they desire as well. Not having what we want and not listening to our heart means teaching others that they, too, should also ignore the music in their heart. This is just another angelic lesson in expansion and contraction. We are either cocreating in expansion or cocreating in contraction. Wouldn't it be amazing if we could all cocreate in expansion? We can practice right now. Just listen to your heart, find its song, and dance your way to a life filled with beauty that is perfect and right for you.

Visualization/Meditation from Haniel:
Tuning In to Positivity

In this guided meditation, you will be able to connect with Archangel Haniel and the vibrational energy of 333. There is no wrong or right way to experience this energy. It will show up differently for each of you. For some, you may feel sensations throughout your body, heat, cold, or even as if something or someone is touching your face. You may even feel a tingling sensation around your head as you move through the meditation script. For others, you might see colors, or your senses may become heightened. Some of you may feel nothing the first time you do this or maybe even the second or third time. Just know that regardless of what does or does not happen to you, Haniel is there with you and will hold sacred space for you to explore all that comes up during your focused and intentional time together. Make sure you do this meditation somewhere quiet where you will not be disturbed. You will need a pink candle, as this color corresponds to the heart, and have it burning throughout the meditation. This candle will help you focus and settle your mind at both the beginning and the end of the meditation. Just remember to blow it out once you are done. You can record this script and listen to it so you can close your eyes, or you can simply keep your eyes open and read through the words. Either way, you will connect with energy and it will benefit you.

For this meditation, you will need to select a piece of music that you find motivational and uplifting. Select this song because of the words. The words need to be positive, life affirming, and empowering. If you are struggling to find a song that does not have sad, angry, or fearful lyrics, by all means pick a mantra instead. There are plenty to choose from on both Spotify or YouTube. I highly recommend "Guru Ram Das" by White Sun. Once you have selected your song or mantra, go ahead and press play and have this song or mantra on a loop as you light your pink candle and settle yourself down to meditate. Focus on the flame and just listen to the words of the song while taking slow, deep, and long breaths. As you breathe, drop your shoulders and feel the tension melt away from your neck and upper back. Watch the flame of your candle as you breathe, and allow yourself to relax as much as possible, letting the music and the words of your song or mantra play away in the background, shifting your energy. Once you feel nice and focused, relaxed, and settled into the moment, let your mind shift to focus on the music. Really listen to the words. Feel the beat. Let it move through your body, and maybe even sway slightly. Do not let your mind shift off the song, and if it helps you stay focused, you can sing along. Do this for a couple of recitations, meaning listen to this song two or three times, then just bring your mind and your focus back onto the flame. Take slow, deep, long breaths as you bring yourself back to the moment and back to the room. Feel the heaviness of your body as it sits on the meditation cushion or on the chair you are seated in. When you feel yourself ready to get up and get on with your day, blow out your candle and turn the music off.

This simple meditation, which is really intentional listening, connects you to the energy of 333 and Archangel Haniel. It will bring you into a state of joy and give your aura a boost of radiance.

Setting Up an Altar to 333 and Archangel Haniel

This altar is for you to focus your energy when you know it is time to open yourself up to joy, love, and fun. You may even want to reset your vibes by intentionally working with 333. Bringing in the energy of 333 and Archangel Haniel will help hold the space for more play in your life. Once you have found an image of Haniel to place on your altar, go ahead and write 333 and a personal prayer to her on a piece of paper. You can do this by hand, print it up, or do it in fancy calligraphy; it is entirely up to you. This is a personal space. You should decorate it in a way that feels right to you. Other things that you might want to put on your altar include flowers, crystals, salt, water, dirt, and of course, you will need a candle, preferably pink, but you can always use white if you can't find any pink candles. Make sure you set your altar up somewhere it will not be disturbed while you are actively using it. However long you decide to use your altar is entirely up to you. You might feel that you only need to do your prayer once, or you may feel called to do it for ten days. It really is up to you.

Once you have your altar set up, I recommend spraying it with a room clearing spray or giving it a once-over with the smoke of an herb bundle. You might try rosemary, lavender, and rose, as they are highly aligned to the heart chakra. This physical act helps mentally and energetically clear the space and sets it up for your prayer/spellwork.

Once your altar is prepped and ready to begin, take a couple of slow, deep breaths, light your candle, and speak your intention statement out loud, beginning with the words: "I call on Archangel Haniel and the power of 333 to hear my intention and assist me in achieving it in the most harmonious way. May this intention be for my higher good, as well as the good of all those who may be involved in creating this intention." Then, go ahead and read your intention statement/prayer: "My intention/ prayer is ..."

To end the ritual, you can either blow the candle out or leave it burning if it is safe to do so. If you choose to blow your candle out, repeat these words first: "As I blow this candle out, I trust that its smoke carries my intention up to the heavens to be manifested by the Universe. I am ready to receive my asking, and so it is." Next, blow out your pink candle and pick up your journal as you launch into the automatic writing prompts below.

Automatic Writing Prompts

After you have done your prayer work, or even after you have done the visualization, you will notice that your connection to Haniel will be more open and messages and information may be starting to trickle or flow on through to you. These may come in the form of single words, sentences, or even just an inner knowing, or because you are working with Haniel and music, these messages may even come in the form of a song—one that will play in your head and keep repeating itself. If you feel moved to, think about pulling out your journal and capitalizing on this connection. Title your page "Talks with Haniel and the Vibrational Energy Known as 333." If you are familiar with journaling work, go ahead and start writing, as you will know how to feel the nudges of the information as it flows from the number 333 and Archangel Haniel. If you are new to journal work, consider using the writing prompts below to get you started with the process.

1. Haniel, how will I know when you are around?
2. How can I step into my joy today?
3. Why have I struggled in the past to bring the energy of joy, fun, and play into my life?
4. How can I let go of my resistance to play and allow myself to slip into the stream of abundance, joy, and love?
5. How will stepping into the energy of 333 assist me today?

You may find that the prompts themselves get you into a nice writing flow, and before you know it, you have moved beyond them. Just lean into the process, trust that Haniel is guiding your hand, and do not try to make logical sense of anything that comes up initially.

Angel Crystal: Ruby

Rubies are historically connected to wealth, beauty, and royalty. Their red coloring connects them to the root chakra, but they are also connected to the heart chakra, making the ruby a fantastic stone to work with when it comes to embodying heart energy, which aligns to abundance. Rubies can help you drop your resistance to receiving and allow you to be more open to living a heart-based experience. For this exercise, we are going to place this embodiment energy into your ruby—be it in its raw or polished form. To do this, you will need a ruby, a piece of paper, a pen, a red candle for passion and desire, and a lunar calendar. You will need a lunar calendar because you will do this exercise under the energy of a new moon or at least in the two and half days of the new moon phase.

On your paper you are going to write the number 333 at the top and some of your heart's desires in a list below the number. You don't have to write everything in your heart, as you can do this exercise once a month if you choose. For now, see if you can come up with a list of between five and ten desires. Make these true and real desires you have—desires that burn with the heat, passion, and intensity of your red candle. There is no place for realism or limitation here. Your ruby stone, 333, and Haniel know no such thing as limit or doubt. So really go for it. It might help to place your ruby in your hand and then place it on your heart while taking a few breaths to open yourself up to hear what your heart and not your head is saying. Don't rush this, take your time, and just sit for as long as you need to. Once you have your list, wrap your ruby in the paper and place it on your Haniel and 333 altar. Go ahead and light your red candle and call in Archangel Haniel. Ask her to infuse your crystal with your heart's desires and to open your ears to the steps that you will need to take and the doors that will now open for you to fulfill these desires. Ask the power of 333 to show up as a reminder to constantly align yourself to the frequency of these heart's desires.

Once you have done your ritual, you can leave your candle burning if it is safe to do so. Otherwise, you can just go ahead and blow it out. Leave your crystal on your altar until the new moon phase is complete, then unwrap it and carry it in your pocket, bra, or purse. This ruby will now become your touchstone to the vibrational power of 333 and your reminder of the angel Haniel, who walks to the beat of your heart. Once your heart's desires have come to pass, you can reset your stone. Just cleanse it first by laying it on a salt tile, giving it some smoke from sage or palo santo, or even laying it out under the full moon. Once it is cleansed, it is ready to be filled up again with your next lot of heart songs.

Additional Number Meanings for Working Haniel's Energy

330—Can you find the joy in things yet to manifest? This number is asking you to do just that. Imagine all that is coming your way and find joy in the knowledge that your angels are bringing it your way at some point in the future.

331—Finding joy in things you do well adds to your manifestation vortex. The more you combine joy and success, the more of it you will have.

332—Tell your spouse, partner, or best friend how much joy they add to your life. Give the gift of joy through the act of love and spread the good vibes around.

334—Take a moment to find joy in the small, often overlooked mundane aspects of your everyday life. It can be easy to take things for granted and to forget that they play a part in a much larger puzzle we call life. Today, recognize the pieces that make up your day and be joyful they are there.

335—It is time to listen to the joyful rhythm of change as it gently blows through your day. This change won't be big, and it may not even be something you would normally notice, but it is there all the same. It could be as simple as taking a new route to work or parting your hair differently. Seek joy in small changes and watch them set the tone for more joyful changes to flow into your life.

336—Today, you are being asked to find the simple pleasures in your local community. Perhaps there is a local garden to visit, a library that is filled with books for you to read, or a local community center that offers you a place to socialize and meet other like-minded people. Whatever it happens to be, rejoice in all the joy your community has to offer.

337—Learning something new can be a fun experience, especially if it is taught the right way. Today, find playful ways to learn something new and watch how it sends a ripple effect out into the other areas of your life.

338—Sometimes the things that bring us the most joy are small and simple, such as a single wildflower, a postcard from a friend, a thank-you email from a client, or a photo of you and people you love. When you see this number, you are being reminded that not everything in your life has to be a major event. Instead, keep it simple and keep it fun.

339—What is your fondest memory? Bring it to the forefront of your mind and allow it to fill you up, bring a smile to your face and a sway to your hip. Hold it for as long as you can, and then get on with the rest of your day.

5

444 ~ ARCHANGEL SAMAEL
Shed the Lens
of Ego Limitations

"The ego is constantly focused on what it
doesn't have or what might be taken from it,
and this limits your vision, blinding you to
the blessings of the Divine all around you."

Deeper Meaning of 444

The angel number 444 reminds us that we have one of two ways
of looking at the world around us: we can either see it as something that is always lacking, or we can see it filled with blessings.
When 444 shows up, it is asking you to stop and question how
you view your world, your life, and your current experience. The
angel number 444 gently nudges us to drop the lens of the ego
so we can see the blessings the Divine provides for us in each

and every moment. For when we look for blessings, we will keep finding them, and this keeps us in a vortex of blessed energy. However, when we view the world and our lives through the lens of lack, we will continue to find things lacking. This leads to feeling left out, disconnected, neglected, and left behind. Archangel Samael wants to pull the ego's lens off your eyes and allow the glory of the Divine into your field of vision.

No matter who we are or where we are, there is always a blessing to be found. It could be as simple as you are alive and that despite everything that has happened to you, you are still choosing to carry on. Perhaps you are surrounded by blessings but you have started to take them for granted. This happens more often than not in first-world experiences. It is easy for those of us who are blessed with choice, options, and convenience to start to take these things for granted and stop seeing them as the blessings they are. The angel number 444 pulls us back to the mundane, to the everyday, to the slow, quiet blessings that surround us, from the wind rustling through the leaves on nearby trees, to the sun shining down on your face, to the clean water that runs when you turn your taps on. Indoor plumbing is a divine blessing, and it is something many in the world don't have.

The next time 444 flashes before your eyes, quickly start listing your blessings. Don't worry about their size or whether you think they are special, just list them. Start simple and stay focused on what surrounds you. Keeping it simple is key to really harnessing the power of 444. Archangel Samael wants you to get back to basics and to stop looking around at the latest and greatest flashing distraction. Instead, move back to the magic of the ordinary, the overlooked, the missed, the magic that happens in the gaps of the distractions.

Right now, in this moment, can you look around you and find ten blessings?

As I write this chapter, I know I am blessed to have a functioning laptop, time to write, a quiet house, internet, a desk to write on, beautiful trees outside my window, a cup of cool, clean water to keep me hydrated, working hands and fingers, a mind that can keep these ideas flowing, and of course, the seat that supports me as I work. These are all blessings. They are items that the Divine has supplied for me so I can show up and be of service and do my job to complete my mission. All of those things may not seem like much, but without them, you would not be reading this book. The angel number 444 is the sum of small things—the way the blessings add up, like a snowball. The more you begin to notice them, the more you will seem to have. The best part is, the more you harness this 444 energy, the more blessings you will create, receive, and be blessed with.

The Angel Samael

Samael is not one of the more common angels; well, not in his true angelic forms, anyway. His many incarnations have him linked to the fallen angels. But according to Samael himself, this is a case of mistaken identity. Like a lot of information from ancient texts, things get lost in translation, leading us to information that may not be accurate. Through my own work with Samael, I have learned that it is his job to offer you true sight, corrective surgery if you will, to cure you of your blindness to all of your divine blessings. This is why, for this book, he is the ruler of 444. In nonreligious practice, Samael is a fantastic archangel to work with when you have lost your way in the world of physical things, are drowning in material possessions, or are sinking in a lack of energy. He is the one who will throw you a lifeline, offer you a hand, and bring you to the shore of the Divine. However, don't think he is going to offer you help if you don't ask for it. He will just sit and watch you suffer. Funny how Samael gets a bad rap for this when in reality this is how all guides work. None of them interfere without permission, yet Samael seems to always be the pinup boy for standing on the sidelines of suffering and just watching it play out.

The truth is all angels do this, without exception, and you know why? It's because we have free will. We have free will to suffer. It is our choice, just as it is our choice to see our blessings, to see ourselves as a blessing, and to lean into Samael and allow him to pull us out of our karmic loop of suffering, lack, and separation. Allowing Samael to work with you through the number 444, you can bring massive change into your life even if it initially feels small and almost unnoticeable. Trust 444 to move your field of vision incrementally, to slowly change your point of focus and guide your mind to perceive the world and your place in it differently. So, the next time you see 444, welcome Archangel Samael into your energy and allow him to show you the blessings you have overlooked. Let him guide you away from the overwhelm and panic and into the flow of feeling connected, worthy, and purposeful.

Visualization/Meditation from Samael: Clearing Your Vision to See Your Blessings

In this guided meditation, you will be able to connect with Archangel Samael and the vibrational energy of 444. There is no wrong or right way to experience this energy. It will show up differently for each of you. For some, you may feel sensations in your body, heat, cold, or even as if something or someone is touching your face and head as you move through the meditation script. For others, you might see colors, or your senses may become heightened. Some of you may feel nothing the first time you do this or maybe even the second or third time. Just know that regardless of what does or does not happen to you, Samael is there with you and will hold sacred space for you to explore all that will become visible to you. Make sure you do this meditation somewhere quiet where you will not be disturbed. If you feel called to, you can light a white candle and have it burning throughout the meditation. Just remember to blow it out once you are done. You can record this script and listen to it so you can close your eyes, or you can simply keep your eyes open and read through the words. Either way, you will connect with energy and it will benefit you.

Do what is most comfortable for you.

Let us begin.

You can be seated or lying down, just do not allow yourself to fall asleep. You may also light some incense if you feel called to do so. Get comfortable and make sure that your head is tilted up. Even if you are lying on the ground or in bed, tilt your chin up. Just focus on your breath, breathing in through the nose and out through the mouth. Keep the breath long and slow as you allow yourself to relax, dropping your shoulders and feeling the tension leave your body with each exhale. Staying focused on the breath, feel yourself dropping further into a relaxed state as you inhale the energy of peace and calm while you exhale stress, anxiety, and tension. As you continue to relax, you may close your eyes, remembering that this is a relaxed state and not a sleeping one. Even though your body is relaxed, your mind will be active and engaged throughout this entire process. As you breathe slowly and deeply, inhale peace and exhale any resistance. Imagine a beautiful golden light flowing into the top of your head, feeling warm, like you're standing under a shower.

Imagine this golden light flowing over your head, down your face, down your neck and shoulders, through your arms, down through the chest and the stomach, and into the pelvis. Then, feel it flowing into the hips, moving down the legs, over the knees, then moving further down your body over your calves and shins, spreading into the ankles, relaxing the arches of your feet, and out the tips of your toes. Feel this golden light as it pours into your body like a wave of energy, filling and lighting you up and connecting you to the energy of Archangel Samael and the power of 444. As you breathe, allow this light to wash through you and ask Archangel Samael to rid you of any illusions of sight that you may be carrying. Ask him to strip away any false lenses that aren't revealing your true divine blessings. Ask him to give you true sight, your natural divine sight, understanding that with this new vision you are calling in you will only be able to see the blessings around you, the abundance of opportunity, and the miraculous flow of possibility from this moment on.

Everywhere you look will be filled with the energy of blessed abundance, wealth, health, happiness, joy, and love. With this new sight, you will come to the realization that it was here all the time and that your true divine blessings have been hiding in plain sight all along. This new vision will show you that you were not disconnected from your divine abundance, but rather you were merely looking at it through a murky and distorted lens. Take your time, focus on your breath, and allow the golden light to flow through your body as Archangel Samael changes your vision, clears and heals your sight, and shifts your sense of perception. Breathe and relax. When you feel that you are complete or you feel that Archangel Samael's energy has stopped flowing through you, focus back on the breath, breathing in peace, calm, and love and breathing out any lingering resistance. Know that you are now infused with the golden energy of Archangel Samael and 444, your sight has now been aligned with divine sight, and everywhere you go, you will always be blessed by an angel. Bring your focus back to your body as you slowly disconnect from the meditative space. With each inhale, ground further into your body. With each exhale, slowly disconnect from the meditative state. Stay with the breath work until you feel fully aware and ready to open your eyes and get on with the rest of your day.

Setting Up an Altar to 444 and Archangel Samael

When you set this altar up, remember that it is going to be your altar for blessings or, more to the point, something to help you see your blessings. One way to do this is to create some blessing jars and place them on your altar. One could be filled with coins to remind you of money blessings. Another could be filled with pictures of loved ones to remind you of your heart blessings, and one could be full of blessings you wish to manifest as a reminder of all the blessings still to come your way. Things you will need for your blessings altar include a picture of Samael or an oracle card, a green candle, 444 written on a green piece of paper, some salt, a pinch of dirt, some feathers, and anything else you feel you want to place upon the altar. You will also want to sit down and compose a prayer or intention statement to Samael and 444. An example might be: "Samael, I am ready to see my blessings, so open my eyes and constantly remind me of all the ways I have been blessed, am blessed, and will be blessed. I allow you to slowly and lovingly open my heart and shower me with as many blessings as I can handle."

Once you have your altar set up, I recommend cleansing it with either a spray or the smoke of some dried sage leaves, just to mentally clear the space and set it up for your prayer work. Then, take a couple of nice deep breaths, light your candle, and speak your intention statement out loud, beginning with the words: "I call on Archangel Samael and the power of 444 to hear my intention and assist me in achieving it in the most blessed way. May my intention be for my higher good, as well as the good of all those who may be involved in making this intention come true." Next, go ahead and read your intention statement/ prayer: "My intention/prayer is ..."

To end the ritual, you can either blow the candle out or leave it burning if it is safe to do so. If you choose to blow your candle out, repeat these words first: "As I blow this candle out, I trust that its smoke carries my intention up to the heavens to be manifested by the Universe. I am ready to receive my asking, and so it is." Now, blow out your candle.

Keep a journal handy over the next few days to document any and all blessings that come your way. Big or small, they all count. Oftentimes we overlook a blessing because we expect it to look or feel different than how it shows up. Now that you have done your prayer and have your altar set up, you will start to notice things you did not before. Recording them in your journal is a way of refining your sight and keeping in the flow of divine vision.

Automatic Writing Prompts

After you have done your prayer work, or even after you have done the visualization, you will notice that your connection to Samael will be more open and blessings will be starting to trickle into your life as well as messages or nudges from Samael and 444. These may come in the form of single words, sentences, or even just an inner knowing. If you feel moved to, think about pulling out your journal and capitalizing on this connection. Title your page "Talks with Samael and the Vibrational Energy Known as 444." If you are familiar with journaling work, go ahead and start writing, as you will know how to feel the nudges of the information as it flows from the number 444 and Archangel Samael. If you are new to journal work, consider using the writing prompts below to get you started with the process:

1. Samael, how will I know when you are around?
2. Where am I allowing myself to get distracted by lack in my life?
3. Why have I struggled in the past to connect with the blessings in my everyday life?
4. How can I become more aware of the way the Divine blesses my life?
5. How will stepping into the energy of 444 assist me today?

You may find that the prompts themselves get you into a nice writing flow, and before you know it, you have moved beyond them. Just lean into the process, trust that Samael is guiding your hand, and do not try to make logical sense of anything that comes up initially.

Angel Crystal: Jade

Jade is considered the crystal of good luck and good fortune. It helps open the heart and allows it to receive. It is often used to bring money, abundance, and self-sufficiency into one's life. You could say it is the crystal of blessings. Jade allows you to feel safe to open up and to be seen so you can be blessed. Let's face it, you need to ask, be heard, and be seen in order to receive, yet so many people ask then hide, run away, and contract. They wonder why nothing shows up. Jade helps keep you open and makes you feel protected enough to stay in the light of the Divine long enough to have good fortune come your way. This makes it the perfect stone to ground the energy of 444 into.

For this exercise, you will need a pen, a piece of paper, a rubber band, a piece of jade (you can even use jewelry with jade in it), and a timer. On the piece of paper, write the number 444, and write it so it fills up the paper, then wrap it around your crystal or piece of jewelry. Secure it with the rubber band. Set your timer to two minutes and get into a nice comfortable position, preferably seated on the floor. If that is not possible, just make sure your back is erect and extended nice and tall with your shoulders back. Place your jade in your right hand and then place your hand on your heart. Lay your left hand on your left knee, palm open and facing up. Once you have established your pose, hit the timer and get back into the pose.

Repeat the following mantra until your timer goes off: "I am blessed, I am."

If you feel moved to, you can repeat this for forty-four days, but just know it is not necessary. Once you feel your jade has been activated and has the full power of 444 in it, start carrying around this pocket stone or start wearing your piece of jewelry. This crystal is now your 444 talisman. It will connect you instantly to the vibration of 444 and all the blessings that Samael wants to illuminate in your life.

Additional Numbers for Working with Samael's Energy

440—There are unlimited opportunities to create more blessings all around you. Right now, count the blessings you are yet to see, the ones you know in your heart are on their way. Be grateful now for what is yet to come.

441—Something new is about to come into your life. See it as a blessing and don't question it. Just allow yourself to receive it with an open heart.

442—You are blessed to have relationships in your life that allow you to be yourself. There are people who truly love you for you. Acknowledge their importance in your life and send a blessing to them right now.

443—Being free to go where you want, when you want is a blessing. Acknowledge your freedoms today and bless them.

445—Change is a blessing as long as it isn't looked at with judgment. A change is coming into your life, and it is bringing a blessing along with it. All it asks is that you don't try and figure out if the change itself is going to be "good" or "bad." Just allow it to be and watch as it unfolds.

446—You are a blessing. How you are right now in this moment as you see this number is a blessing. Your very existence is a blessing. You do not need to do anything in order to just be a blessing.

447—Some blessings bring lessons with them. In fact, some blessings wrap themselves in a cloak of wisdom. Now is one of those times. So count your blessings and wait and see what pieces of sage advice they offer.

448—Material items are blessings; they aren't the only blessings, but they are blessings. A lot of times we forget how blessed we are, but when you see this number, list and count your material blessings.

449—Being able to let things go is a blessing. Saying goodbye and allowing things to come to their natural end is a part of the blessing cycle. Rejoice today in the endings around you and bless them for what they are: gateways to something new.

6

555 ~ ARCHANGEL URIEL
Let Go and
Trust the Change

"Change is the only constant you will have
in your physical experience, so make
it your friend and invite it in."

Deeper Meaning of 555

Change: you either love it or you hate it. Problem is, you can't
stop it. The angel number 555 marks a time of change. It could
be big, it could be small, but change is happening whether you
like it or not. Nothing in the physical or vibrational world stays
the same. Change is constant. It is a universal law. The angel
number 555 is merely a reminder that this law will be played out
in your life regardless of your emotions, thoughts, or beliefs. You
need not be ready for it or even accept it. It just is. Archangel

Uriel wants you to think of 555 as a courtesy call from the Universe, a note from God if you will, that things in your life won't be staying the same, cycles are spinning, time is moving, and the path has changed direction.

Sometimes when this number pops up, you don't notice anything in your outside world. Nothing you can perceive with your five limited senses appears to be any different. However, change has happened, and eventually your outer world will catch up. Other times, 555 will stalk you. It will be everywhere you go. It will be all you see, hear, and notice. This sort of constant repetition is like an alarm, one even your limited senses cannot ignore. This is the sign of bigger shifts and grander plans being adjusted. This is where your outer world will feel the jolt. Regardless of where this change happens, inside of you or outside of you, it has happened. You cannot wish it away. You cannot deny it. You can't explain it away. The angel number 555 is your sign. It is your note from the higher realms, and it clearly says, "Change is happening." It is important to note that this change won't be delayed. It won't be something that might or could happen in the distant future. It is happening right now as you are seeing the numbers, and Archangel Uriel is smack in the middle of it.

Just as cyclic time must continue to change the seasons, you must also experience change, a difference, a bit of a shake-up. Otherwise, you will fall into stagnation, which leads to illness. Lack of movement slows us down, gets us stuck, and, if prolonged, can make movement difficult. If you never water your plants, if you never adjust the amount of sun they get or don't get, they will die. You are exactly the same. The conditions in your physical experience constantly change, and you need to adjust and change along with them. You could say 555 is also the number of adaptability. Those that adapt, thrive, and those who dig in their heels, suffer. Although seeing 555 means change is upon you, it also gives you the chance to decide how you wish to handle it and how you will manage your mind, your emotions, and your levels of resistance. The angel number 555 alerts you to your free will, the part of you that only you have control over.

So, how will you use your free will when 555 flashes into your life?

This is where calling on Archangel Uriel can be helpful, as you can give over your worry, your fear, and your struggle to him. You can ask him to take it from you and keep you free to flex and adapt. No one said you have to do this alone. Call on Uriel when you see 555, and ask him to stand with you, to hold you, support you, and steady you as the laws of the Universe unfold in your life. These are the sorts of tasks he was created for. Standing on the edge of the unknown, steadying your shaky legs, and being there when everyone else walks away is Archangel Uriel's superpower. He will stay by your side and offer you as much unconditional love as you can take. The angel number 555 lets you know change is inevitable, but Archangel Uriel reminds you it doesn't mean you have to suffer.

The Angel Uriel

Uriel is my personal angel. Unlike all the other angels in this book, he is the one I know intimately, which means in this section, I am going to introduce you to the Uriel I know and the Uriel that has been a huge part of my life for over a decade. So let me apologize in advance if what I write here does not gel with anything you have read or your own personal experience with Uriel. Uriel, for the most part, is considered an angel of transformation, often referred to as the archangel who shepherds the recently dead from the earth plane and delivers them to the other world. I guess, in some respects, this is true. He is happy to take people who have entered into the death phase of their lives and help them find a new path.

Yet, here in 555, we very rarely speak of physical death but refer to the death of a cycle or life phase. We experience many deaths while we live. We die every night and come to life every morning. Death is the ultimate change, the most powerful of all transformations, and Uriel stands at the precipice of these changes. He sees something beautiful in the spaces where others only see broken and decayed things. He will reach in and breathe new life into situations, places, and people. He and 555 could just as easily be called "the breath of new life" as they could be called "change." There is no denying that wherever Uriel is, something is coming to an end so something new can come into being. Hanging with Uriel for over a decade has taught me how nice change is and how enjoyable it can be. How miraculous it is to invite into your life, like a good friend. I have let go of my need to suffer through change, and I have dropped my worry and fear about what will be waiting on the other side of change. Uriel has instead instilled me with excitement and expectancy. He has allowed me to see the sheer necessity of this law. Uriel has made me so comfortable with the energy of change and its cyclic nature that now I get worried when I don't see 555.

We hope that by the time you finish with the exercises in this chapter, you will look forward to seeing these numbers as well. In fact, we want you to get so comfortable with them, that you call on them on purpose. Uriel wants to bring change into your life. He wants to introduce you to the magic and majesty of your power. However, in order to do this, you must embrace the cycles of your life, the endings and the beginnings, and the law of change. The more you work with Uriel and the energy of 555, the more flexible and adaptable you will be. You will let go of things more easily. You will release attachments to people, places, and things that do not align to your true self, and you will allow Uriel to set your feet on the path of transformation without fear or doubt because you will trust that whatever is waiting for you along the path has been handpicked by the angels just for you to experience.

Visualization/Meditation: Helping You Transform into the Change You Want to See in Your Life

In this guided meditation, you will be able to connect with the transformative energy of Archangel Uriel. Just know there is no wrong or right way to experience this energy. It will show up differently for each of you. For some, you may feel sensations in your body, heat, or cold, and you may even feel like a feather is gently stroking your face or head as you move through this meditation script. For others, you might see colors, or your senses may become heightened. Some of you may feel nothing the first time you do this or maybe even the second or third time. Don't worry; it is completely normal. Just know that regardless of what does or does not happen to you, Uriel is there with you, protecting you and holding space for you to explore the change you wish to create in your life. Make sure you do this meditation somewhere quiet where you will not be disturbed. If you feel called to, you can light a golden candle and have it burning throughout the meditation. Just remember to blow it out once you are done. You can record this script and listen to it so you can close your eyes, or you can simply keep your eyes open and read through the words. Either way, you will connect with energy and it will benefit you.

Do what is most comfortable for you.

Let us begin.

Go ahead and get comfortable. If it is safe to do so, lie down or recline in your favorite chair. If it helps you to focus, pull out your meditation cushion and get into your favorite pose. Take three deep grounding breaths in through the nose and out through the mouth. As you inhale, think the word "peace," and as you exhale, think the word "transform." Keep this breath work going for a couple of minutes, breathing in "peace," and breathing out "transform." With each breath, allow yourself to become more and more relaxed and to sink deeper and deeper into this moment and into the rhythm of your breath work. Continue concentrating on the mantra "peace" and "transform." Allow your shoulders to drop, let your hips settle, and give yourself permission to breathe deeper and longer. As you fall into a state of calm and openness, and continuing to be focused on the breath work, call in Archangel Uriel and ask him to sit behind you.

Gently lean back into his embrace, feeling the warmth that radiates out of his body into yours, allowing you to sink even deeper into peace and calm. Here, in the arms of Archangel Uriel, bring to mind an area of your life that you know needs to be changed or needs to have the energy around it transformed. Just allow the image of this area of your life to appear, doing your best to not attach to any of the feelings or emotions that may arise as you shift your focus to this area of your current experience. Instead, breathe out any fear or anxiety and give it to Uriel so that he can transform it into love, peace, and relief. He will then give it back to you as he radiates heat from his body to yours.

Keep up the breath work, breathing out the fear and breathing in the love knowing that you are supported and knowing that Uriel has you in his arms throughout this entire process. Continue the process until you feel a sense of relief, which may feel like the loosening of the muscles in your body or the lessening of the feeling of anxiety in your mind. It may also mean that the thought of this area of your life no longer seems to have an emotional charge. Just keep breathing, giving all over to Uriel, until you find the relief. When you are done and feel this sense of relief, however it has shown up for you, bring to mind 555. Now, ask for it to change, transmute, and transform this area of your life right now, in this moment, as you feel this sense of relief. Stay in this state for as long as you need to, allowing both Uriel and the power of 555 to work their magical change in your life. Keep breathing and sink deeper into Uriel's arms.

When you are done or feel a sense of completion, just focus back on your breath work, letting the image of the number 555 drop away slowly. Feel yourself detaching from Uriel as you thank him for being your support, your guide, and your change agent today. Bring the breath work back to the mantra "peace" and "transform" as you ground yourself back into your body. Let yourself become more aware of your physical surroundings with each inhale, becoming more alert, focused, aware, strong, steady, and confident. When you are ready, open your eyes if you had them closed. Stretch out your arms, roll your shoulders, wiggle your fingers and your toes, and then take a nice quiet moment before you go and get on with the rest of your day.

Setting Up an Altar to 555 and Archangel Uriel

If you know you are ready to bring change into your life, then setting up an altar to ground the energy of 555 and Archangel Uriel is the way to go. To set this altar up, you will need a yellow candle (as this is the color we connect to the action center of your body: the solar plexus), a sunstone crystal, a picture of Uriel, the number 555 written or printed out on yellow paper, and a very clear intention statement of the change you wish to call in. This intention statement should also explain why this change is important to you and the steps you will take once you notice that change is afoot. You can also add other elements to your altar such as feathers, salt, soil, pictures, or whatever calls to you. Make sure you set your altar up somewhere it will not be disturbed while you are actively using it. However long you decide to use your altar is entirely up to you. You may feel that you only need to do your prayer once, or you may feel called to do it for fifty-five days. It really is up to you.

Once you have your altar set up, I recommend spraying it with a sage spray or giving it a once-over with the smoke of palo santo. This will mentally and energetically clear the space and set it up for your prayer work. Once your space is clear and ready, take a couple of nice deep breaths, light your candle, and speak your intention statement out loud, beginning with the words: "I call on Archangel Uriel and the power of 555 to hear my intention and assist me in achieving it in the most surprising way. May my intention be for my higher good, as well as the good of all those who may be involved in bringing my intention into being." Then read your intention statement/prayer: "My intention/prayer is ..."

To end the ritual, you can either blow the candle out or leave it burning if it is safe to do so. If you choose to blow your candle out, repeat these words first: "As I blow this candle out, I trust that its smoke carries my intention up to the heavens to be manifested by the Universe. I am ready to receive my asking, and so it is." Now, blow out your candle.

Your job now is to stay open, observe, and act as if the change you have asked for is being created in your life.

Automatic Writing Prompts

After you have done your prayer work or even after you have done the visualization, you may notice that your connection to Uriel will be starting to open. This may mean messages and information will begin to trickle through you. Consider pulling out your journal and capitalizing on this connection. Title your page "Talks with Uriel and the Vibrational Energy Known as 555." You can then just start writing if you are somewhat used to journaling work. If you are not a journaling person or this sort of writing is new to you, consider using these writing prompts to get you started and more familiar with the process:

1. Uriel, how will I know when you are around?
2. What area of my life is 555 affecting right now and why?
3. Why have I been scared of change in the past, and how can I shift my thoughts and beliefs around change?
4. What action steps can I take today to move me closer to letting go of my fear and resistance when it comes to change?
5. How will stepping into the energy of 555 assist me today?

Angel Crystal: Sunstone

When we are in the dark, we seek light. When we are knee-deep in the unknown, we reach for hope. When change weakens us at the knees, we pray for strength. Sunstone brings the energy, vitality, and light of the sun to all your moments of change and transformation. It will uplift you, energize you, and show you there were never any monsters hiding under the bed. This makes sunstone the perfect crystal to ground the energy of 555 and Archangel Uriel.

To infuse your crystal, you are going to need a piece of paper, a pen, and a rubber band or small piece of tape. Your piece of paper needs to be big enough to wrap your crystal in. I recommend a nice pocket stone, but the size is entirely up to you. Just make sure your paper can cover your crystal completely, wrapping it like a present. On the inside of the paper, write the number 555 five times. You should not be able to see the writing once you wrap your crystal. Next, wrap your crystal, securing the paper with either a piece of tape or a rubber band. These next few steps you are going to do over a four-day period, moving the crystal into a different place each evening. Simply, you are going to infuse your sunstone with the energy of the sunrise from the four directions, starting in the east, moving to the south, then the west, and ending with the north.

Now, if you live in an apartment or flat that doesn't give you access to all four directions, you might have to get creative about this. At the time of writing this book, I was living in an apartment that only had westerly facing windows and a small balcony that barely gave me southern and northern aspects. I had no access to eastern sunrises. So, while I was working through this exercise for this book, I used my car by moving the crystal around the back window to get the westerly, easterly, northerly, and southerly energy I needed. I could have also asked a friend of mine if I could have done it in her front garden, but my car just seemed so much easier. So, don't fret if you have limited windows; you will find an easy way to infuse your crystal.

Each evening you are going to place your crystal either in a window, on a balcony, somewhere in your garden or, like I had to, in the car. You will retrieve your crystal by midday each day, if possible. If not, that's fine; just make sure you move it before the next sunrise. Once your crystal is in place and will get full sun the coming morning, recite the following prayer:

> *I call on the power of 555 and Archangel Uriel to infuse my sunstone with the power, ease, grace, and joy of change. With the four directions to guide me, I know I will always be pointed in the right direction and headed down the correct path, as I am guided by the flow of transformation. I give thanks to the sunrise, as it reminds me that all things begin again, and in order for that to happen things need to constantly move and change. Uriel and 555, bless my crystal, bless me and keep me in your protective embrace, and so it is.*

Once you have the energy of all the directions infused into your sunstone, unwrap it and put it in your pocket, bra, or bag, as you are good to go and flow with all the new changes about to unfold in your life.

Additional Numbers for
Working with Uriel's Energy

550—When one welcomes change into their lives, they also welcome multiple possible futures and an exciting number of opportunities.

551—It is time to change the way you view your personal magic. You are a powerful creator, so allow yourself to transform any area of our life in which you don't feel satisfied. Just wave your magic wand and see the change happen.

552—There is a relationship in your life that is ready to transform into something different. It could be with another person, it could be a creative project, or it could even be with yourself.

553—All work and no play makes you a very boring person indeed. It's time to change the structure of your daily life so you can bring more play and fun into your routine.

554—Sometimes limit and discipline is a good thing. Right now you are being asked to change the way you view both of these things in your life. Uriel says, "Where there was once a negative, there is now a positive."

556—What part of yourself have you not been loving the way it truly deserves to be loved? Now is the time to find that part of you and change your thoughts and feelings around how you view it, speak to it, and embrace it.

557—Learning new skills is a great way to welcome change into your life. Sign up for a new class or group coaching program and let the new energy sweep through your life.

558—Everything in the physical world changes. There is not one aspect that ever stays the same. When you fear what is coming next, think about nature and how easily it allows change in order to let life force energy flow.

559—All endings bring change, and the one you now face is no different. Just keep in mind that this ending is laying the groundwork for an amazing transformation to take place.

666 ~ ARCHANGEL ARIEL
Love Thyself as We Love You

"Self-love is the greatest gift you can give your-self, for when you love yourself, you show the rest of the world how to love you as well."

Deeper Meaning of 666

The word "love" is thrown around a lot in the human realm, yet many humans don't know what divine love is, nor do they love themselves the way the Divine or the angels do. The energy of divine love is in its purest form when you can love yourself the way the angels love you—when you can live as love, be love, and live life from your heart not your head. It saddens the angels to see how many humans do not love who they are or feel they need to be someone other than themselves. They see how many humans struggle with being themselves and how humanity in general constantly questions if they are enough, which is why Archangel Ariel wants you to get into the flow of turning love inward through the act of seeing 666.

Can you think about someone or something you love—totally and completely love—without judgment? Perhaps it is another human, a pet, or love for a physical object. This love you have for this other is so pure that it just flows from you without thought. This is the love 666 asks you to turn on yourself, to draw it into your very being and soak it up. Loving yourself and opening yourself to your own love allows you to find out what love really feels like. Love is not something we learn from other people; it is what we learn from how we treat ourselves. When you treat yourself with compassion, others show you compassion. When you treat yourself with kindness, so, too, will those around you. When you can see yourself without judgment, you will no longer judge others. When you turn love inward, you radiate love outward. The angel number 666 is your key to bringing more love not only into your life but into the world at large.

The question 666 asks is, "How much love can you give yourself?" What you give to yourself, you give to the world. The angel number 666 reminds you that love is like breathing: you can't exhale only. At some point, you have to inhale, just as you can't inhale without at some point needing to exhale. You need both an in breath and an out breath. This is also how love works: you take it in and you let it out—self-love, divine love, and love for all. It is as simple as breathing. You don't judge your breath. You don't deem it worthy or undesirable. You do not put conditions around inhaling and exhaling. You just accept it as something you need to survive and do it on instinct. The angel number 666 is your new love habit. It is the sign that loving yourself is as simple and instinctive as breathing. If the angels can teach us humans nothing else, let them teach us at least about love because you do not need to do anything to be loved. You are, therefore you are love. You will be loved, and you will flow that love into the world around you. It will happen without thought, by instinct, and every time you see the number 666.

The Angel Ariel

I remember the first time Ariel came to me via meditation. To be honest, it wasn't the most gracious of meetings. I kept asking her if she was a mermaid spirit, and she kept telling me no. At the time I wasn't overly knowledgeable about angels and just how many of them there were. (For the record, there are hundreds of thousands of them.) Anyhoo, I digress. I had been working with Uriel for about two months when Ariel came into my life. For me, Ariel has similar energy to Uriel, and if I didn't know better, I would say they were the yin and yang of each other. However, the more I worked with them, the more I was able to discern the differences in their energy. If you are new to both of these angels, you can be forgiven for thinking of them as two sides of the same coin. The biggest difference is that Ariel is dedicated to teaching humans how lovable they are. She comes into people's lives to remind them that they are love, not that they need love. It is a huge difference. Even by just saying the sentence out loud, you will notice a difference in the energy. Go ahead and try it. "I am love," then, "I need love." One claims your energy as love, and one holds the vibration of lacking love.

Ariel's job should be the easiest in the world, but she tells me it is often one of the hardest. It breaks her heart to see how many of us humans don't believe that we are lovable. Calling Archangel Ariel into your life is a lesson in self-love. You do not need to be worthy of her for her to show up. You do not need to do or be anything for her to remind you just how much love you already have inside of you. Over the years I have had many clients tell me how unworthy they feel about calling on the angels for help and guidance and that they feel they will be judged and rejected for past deeds. Ariel is your reminder that you don't have to be worthy to be who you already are. You are love. Love and you are one. There is no separation of who you are and the vibrational energy we call love.

"I am love, I am" is your mantra. It is your birthright. Love is the very essence that made you, which pumps through you and carries you from one incarnation to the next. Everything you are, everything you do, and everything you become is a form of love. There is no part of you that is not touched by love, and it is Archangel Ariel's job to remind you of this truth. For it is true, even when we doubt it, push it away, or try to run from it. The point is, when you are love, you can never outrun it, escape it, or be apart from it. You may not always acknowledge it or even feel like you want to own it, but it is you and you are it.

After our first meeting, I worked with Ariel for months healing the many wounds inside my heart chakra. I saw firsthand how terribly I had hurt myself by thinking I was separate from love and by judging my worthiness of love. The scars and gaping sores I was carrying around with me were not because love wasn't available to me but because I held a false belief that I was unlovable. Ariel reminds us that love doesn't need anything to be; it just is. Let it in and you will see just how much like love you truly are.

Visualization/Meditation from Ariel:
Send Love to Yourself

In this guided meditation you will be able to connect with Archangel Ariel and the vibrational energy of 666. Keep in mind that there is no wrong or right way to connect with these energies, for they will show up differently for everyone. Some people may feel sensations in their body, heat, or cold as they do this meditation, while others may feel as if something or someone is touching their face and head as they read through the meditation scripts. Others may see colors or notice their senses have become heightened, and some may feel nothing the first time they do this meditation or maybe even the second or the third. Just know that regardless of what does or does not happen, Ariel is there with you and will hold sacred space for you to explore the loving energy that she brings forth along with the vibrational energy of 666. Make sure you do this meditation somewhere quiet where you will not be disturbed. If you feel called to, you can light a white candle and have it burning throughout the meditation. Just remember to blow it out once you are done. You can record this script and listen to it so you can close your eyes, or you can simply keep your eyes open and read through the words. Either way, you will connect with energy and it will benefit you.

Do what is most comfortable for you.

Let us begin.

For this meditation it's important to think of yourself as if you were another person, someone separate yet connected to yourself. The reason this is important is because we tend to be able to care for others more easily than directing that care toward ourselves. So for this meditation, create a version of yourself that needs the most care. It could be your inner child, it could be the version of yourself that needs physical healing, or it could be the version of yourself that is struggling mentally and emotionally. It could be the version of yourself that is up leveling and needs to be reminded that, even when you are feeling good and pushing yourself, you still need kindness, compassion, support, and uplifting. It doesn't matter which version of yourself you pick as long as you make sure that you are seeing this version of who you are as separate yet connected to you.

Get comfortable, take a couple of slow, deep breaths, and bring this version of yourself to your mind's eye. See this version of yourself in its state of struggle, doubt, expansion, sadness, or pain. Allow yourself to fully take in this version of you and the scene you have created. Where have you placed this version of yourself? What surrounds you in that place? What can you hear, and how do you feel when you look at yourself? As you hold this image in your mind's eye, gather as much information as you can from the scene without becoming attached or emotionally connected. Place your hand on your heart and ask for the energy of 666 and the healing power of Archangel Ariel to flow through you into the scene and to this version of you that needs this self-love and self-care. Watch as this energy moves from your heart into the scene and infuses it with a beautiful pink light. The more energy you can send from your heart chakra and the deeper you can form your connection between 666 and Archangel Ariel, the more light you will infuse into the image within your mind's eye. Remember to breathe as you keep sending this pink light to the you that needs it. Infuse this scene, this image, with as much self-love and self-care as you possibly can. Watch as this other version of yourself openly receives this energy. See how this version of yourself just allows the pink light into their being by breathing it in. See it filling up this version of you from the top of the head to the tips of the toes, making this version of you shine like a bright pink star.

When you feel complete or you feel that the energy has run its course and you can't feel its tug anymore, repeat the words: "Thank you, and I love you" three times before removing your hand from your heart. Take a couple of deep, slow breaths in through the nose and out through the mouth as you bring yourself back to your body, becoming focused and aware, knowing that this version of you, this piece of you that you saw during meditation, is now doing much better than it was before. Keep breathing deeply and slowly until your full awareness comes back to your body in the room, understanding that you are whole, complete, and one with all the pieces of yourself. You can repeat this meditation at any time, and you can direct this energy to any version of yourself you choose. The power of self-love and self-care is literally in your hands.

Setting Up an Altar to 666 and Archangel Ariel

When you set this altar up, remember that this is going to be your altar for self-care and self-love. One way to set this altar up is to place a self-care and self-love vision or mood board on your altar. You can cut as many images out and paste them onto your board as you want. The things you will need for your altar include a picture of Ariel or an oracle card with her picture on it, a red candle to represent pure, deep love, 666 written on a green piece of paper, some salt, a pinch of dirt, some feathers, and anything else you feel you want to place upon the altar to represent self-care and self-love. You will also want to sit down and compose a prayer or intention statement to Ariel and 666. An example might be, "Ariel, I call on you to show me the path to loving myself. Guide me to make loving decisions and open my heart so that I can see myself through your divine eyes."

Once you have your altar set up, I recommend spraying it with a clearing spray or giving it a once-over with the smoke from an herb stick with roses petals in it. This will help clear the space and set it up for your prayer work. Once you have cleansed your altar and are ready to begin, take a couple of nice deep breaths, light your red candle, and speak your intention statement out loud, beginning with the words: "I call on Archangel Ariel and the power of 666 to hear my intention and assist me in achieving it in the most nourishing and nurturing way. May my intention be for my higher good and the good of all those who may be involved in bringing my intention into reality." Then read your intention statement/prayer: "My intention/ prayer is ..."

To end the ritual, you can either blow the candle out or leave it burning if it is safe to do so. If you choose to blow your candle out, repeat these words first: "As I blow this candle out, I trust that its smoke carries my intention up to the heavens to be manifested by the Universe. I am ready to receive my asking, and so it is." Then, blow out your candle.

Your job is now to be alert to any and all offerings of love and devotion that come into your life. Do not judge them or even question their motives. Instead, learn to just say thank you and accept, letting your heart receive without conditions, limitations, and expectations. Trust that Archangel Ariel is flowing in and around the energy that now floats into your life.

Automatic Writing Prompts

After you have done your prayer work, or even after you have done the visualization, you will notice that your connection to Ariel will be more open and messages and information will be starting to trickle or flow through. These may come in the form of single words, sentences, or even just an inner knowing. This makes now a good time to pull out your journal and capitalize on this connection. Title your page "Talks with Ariel and the Vibrational Energy Known as 666." If you are familiar with journaling work, go ahead and start writing, as you will know how to feel the nudges of the information flowing from the number 666 and Archangel Ariel. If you are new to journal work, consider using the writing prompts below to get you started with the process:

1. Ariel, how will I know when you are around?
2. Where in my life do I need to learn more self-love?
3. Why have I struggled in the past to love myself the same way I tend to love others?
4. How can I establish more loving, devotional practices in my daily experience?
5. How will stepping into the energy of 666 assist me today?

You may find that the prompts themselves get you into a nice writing flow, and before you know it, you have moved beyond them. Just lean into the process, trust that Ariel is guiding your hand, and do not try to make logical sense of anything that comes up initially.

Angel Crystal: Rose Quartz

Rose quartz is the crystal of the heart. It resonates to the frequency of unconditional maternal love. This is why so many people find themselves attracted to it. It has a gentle, loving presence to it, which can calm one's nerves, ground one's energy back into their body, and slowly and gently heal one's heart wounds. This makes it the perfect crystal to infuse with the energy of 666 and the gentle, loving radiance of Archangel Ariel. To do that, you will need a rose quartz pocket stone (as you may want to keep this crystal with you often), a piece of paper big enough to wrap your stone in, a rubber band or tape to seal the paper, and a pen. You will also need a pink candle to align to your rose quartz, a photo of yourself, and a timer. Set your timer for two minutes.

To begin, write the number 666 at the top of your paper. Then write the following affirmation statements under it:

"I am love, I am."

"I am the frequency of love."

"I am resonating with love."

"My life is a living prayer to love."

"Every day in every way my life flows with the frequency of divine love."

If you wish to add some more of your own, by all means please do, but know that these five are more than enough. You can decorate your paper if you feel the need to. You can also place pictures of things you love onto the paper, as well as the picture of yourself. Once your paper is ready, place your rose quartz into the middle of it and wrap your stone up, sealing it with either a rubber band or some tape.

Once you have your crystal and your paper completed, go and sit before your Archangel Ariel altar. Place your pink candle upon the altar and light it. Get comfortable and gaze at the flame of the candle. Place your crystal in your hand (it doesn't matter which one) and hold it to your heart. Next, go ahead and hit your timer. For the next two minutes, repeat the words "I love you" over and over again until the timer goes off. You can keep your eyes open and focused on the flame, or if it is easier for you to stay focused on the mantra, close your eyes. When your timer goes off, do not rush to get up. Instead, just sit with your crystal and decide if you are going to keep it wrapped in its bundle or if you are going to unwrap it. There is no right or wrong choice here. Trust how you feel. If you can't seem to decide in that moment, leave it wrapped and place it on your Ariel altar until you need the crystal, and then it will be clear to you how you will work with this stone. You may decide to keep your crystal wrapped, sealing the energy in, or you will know to unwrap it and feel the energy deeply impressed and stored within it. Trust that whichever decision you make is the right one for you, your heart, and how you will work with the energy of 666 and Archangel Ariel.

Additional Numbers for Working with Ariel's Energy

660—The more love you send yourself, the more self-loving opportunities you will see. For once you are in the vortex of your own love, it expands and shows you other ways to express it, create it, and receive it.

661—Be a leader in self-love by finding ways today to show how love can be the most powerful tool you have in your magical tool belt. Send love to your boss, your supervisor, anyone in your life that oversees you or has a higher position than you.

See them surrounded in the same loving energy that you see yourself in.

662—Send love to your past self. Hold an image of yourself in the past in your mind's eye and send it as much love as you can bear. See yourself being bathed in this love as it heals and transforms the painful past-self energy.

663—Send love to your future self. You live in residual energy, meaning that what you experience today is what you set up for yourself weeks, months, or sometimes even years ago. So today, give your future self the gift of love. Pick a future date, visualize yourself at that point in time, and bathe yourself in love. Think how wonderful this energy will be when you get to catch up with it!

664—Set your boundaries with love. Oftentimes we set up walls and boundaries around ourselves as defense mechanisms. These tend to vibrate a lot of fear. When you see this number, it is asking you to tear those walls down and build love boundaries instead. Establish loving limits and restrictions around your life, body, mind, and energy. Doing this as an act of self-love will only allow the very best energy to come back to you.

665—Embrace change lovingly. Hold it in your heart. Tell it you love it and see it bathed in the light of Archangel Ariel, knowing that this change is coming to you straight from the frequency of love itself.

667—Ariel once told me that lessons in life do not have to be hard or harsh. In fact, she says we can ask them to be gentle, kind, and loving. So today, when you see this number, remember that you can request loving lessons rather than hard and fast ones.

668—Love what you have. Love what you have created and love all that you still wish to have. Filling your material world with love means that every exchange you have will be intentional, empowering, and expanding.

669—Take a moment to reflect on the love you have been given over your life. Do not judge the quality or the size of it, just acknowledge that it has been there, is still there, and will always be there. You came from love and to love you will return.

777 ~ ARCHANGEL RAZIEL
The Unknown Is
Your Guide; Trust It

"When you open yourself up to things you
don't know, you find more things to
enrich and expand your life."

Deeper Meaning of 777

Have you ever noticed that the more you know, the more you
realize you don't know? That is the energy of 777. It is the quest
for knowing and the unquenchable thirst for knowledge. In
many respects, 777 is a call to higher learning and to expand
yourself in all ways, not just in a mental way. When 777 comes
into your life, it alerts you to the fact that lessons are afoot. Some
of these may be new lessons or some of them may be old ones,

showing up again to be learned, cleared, and healed. The interesting thing about 777 is that you might be the teacher or you might be the student. There is no division when it comes to 777, which is why we think of this number as the master/student number. For when we are on the path of knowledge, wisdom, and understanding, 777 will come to us whether we are in the role of student or while we are in the role of teacher. You teach to those who are not as far along the path as you are, but you also learn from those who are further along the path than you.

In this respect, 777 shows us how knowledge is a give-and-take. It is a dance between multiple partners, constantly shifting and turning, and you never quite know who or what you will come across next. Each new unknown brings with it a new lesson to learn and a new person to impart some part of your wisdom upon. Archangel Raziel knows that we are constantly exchanging knowledge. We are always in a dialogue with 777, most of the time unknowingly. We teach just by being alive. We learn just by living. This push and pull, give-and-take, yin and yang is the way we traverse the energy of 777. Learning through the unknown is what this journey is all about, as we always find ourselves in a place of receiving or sharing information.

Archangel Raziel asks, "What lesson is trying to get your attention?" To answer this question, just pay attention the next time 777 comes dancing into your life. What situation are you going through at this time? Who is with you? Where are you physically? I used to see 777 on license plates when I would drive to classes or workshops I was teaching. Without fail, every time I would head off to teach, 777 would be right in front of me. It got to the point where I just expected to see it. The fantastic thing is, even though I was the one leading the class or workshop, I always walked away knowing something I never knew I didn't know, which is exactly what 777 brings us: the unknown and the things we didn't know we didn't know. This makes the unknown one of the best guides we have. Archangel Raziel knows this, which is why he loves to flash 777 into our life at just the right time. Think of 777 as Raziel's way of conspiring for your better and highest good. He is illuminating you to something you didn't know but need to know, and to something you would never have sought out because you did not know you didn't know it and needed to know it. Confused yet? Raziel likes to work in riddles and messy zigzagging lines, so don't worry if at this point your head is spinning. Instead, trust that 777 is showing up in your life because you need to know something, such as a lesson, an idea, a shift in perspective, or a teachable moment you never knew you needed until it appears.

The Angel Raziel

Raziel is a trickster, magician, riddle master, and mathematician. He has a way with puzzles, equations, and quests and loves bringing hidden knowledge out into the open. Wherever there is a problem to be solved or something new to be learned, Raziel will be there. When I was first introduced to Raziel, it was when I was trying to come to terms with all my new angel friends. My life had been turned on its head, and I was very much treading the waters of Lake Unknown. I would like to say that Raziel was there to throw me a lifeline, but that's not really his style. He is more the type of angel who stands on the shore and throws questions at you while you are trying to learn to swim. You see, Raziel won't just hand you answers. He likes to create the conditions in which you will find your own answers, have your own breakthroughs, and find your own way back to the shore. This archangel is not about perfection; he is about results. The messier the equation, the clumsier the attempt at finding your own solution, the happier Raziel is, which is one of the keys to working with this angel and the energy of 777.

Trusting the unknown isn't meant to be pretty. There are no elegant ways to learn what you don't know. It is all trial and error. It's about getting things wrong before you get them right. The point is, when Raziel comes knocking, you can pretty much guarantee that life is about to get very interesting. So, put on some comfy clothes, put your hair up, and prepare to get your hands dirty. This is not about being ready or being mentally or spiritually prepared. You will be thrown from your comfort zone, and Raziel will look you deep in your soul and ask you to have faith. He asks you to have faith in what is happening, what is being revealed, and that the mess and confusion is all leading you down the path of knowledge, answers, and solutions. In many ways this is liberating, as there is no wrong or right way to work with 777 and Archangel Raziel. When 777 comes into your life, it is time to locate the places in your life where things are being turned on their heads. It may even be an area of your life that feels out of control or overwhelming. This is where you will find Archangel Raziel.

Now, don't get me wrong, he does not create the chaos; he just thrives on finding the pieces of information required to calm the storm and return you and all those involved to a new sense of normal. This is part of knowing what you never knew you didn't know. Once you have identified this area of your life, it is time to take the first step of your journey with 777 and Raziel, which is to surrender. Let go of everything you think you know. When one can empty one's mind, one clears a space for new things to pour in. The emptier you can be, the more you can be filled up with the knowledge and understanding that both Raziel and 777 can bring you.

Visualization/Meditation from Raziel: Opening up to Answers, Solutions, and New Information

In this guided meditation you will be able to connect with Archangel Raziel and the vibrational energy of 777. This meditation is to help you connect with the frequency of knowledge, wisdom, and understanding. It can also be used to eliminate any fear or doubt you may be carrying. This fear-based energy could very well be a point of resistance to opening yourself up to learn something new. It could also be blocking an answer to a question or the solution to a problem from coming into your life. This meditation can also help you shift your focus and your mind away from a problem and allow the unseen to become visible. There is no wrong or right way to experience this energy. It will show up differently for each of you. For some, you may feel sensations in your body, heat, cold, or even feel as if something or someone touches your face and head as you move through the meditation script. You might see colors, or your senses may become heightened. You also may feel nothing the first time you do this or maybe even the second or third time. Just know that regardless of what does or does not happen to you, Raziel is there with you and will hold sacred space for you to explore all that will become visible to you. Make sure you do this meditation somewhere quiet and where you will not be disturbed. If you feel called to, you can light a blue candle, as blue is the color of the throat chakra, the center of communication, and have it burning throughout the meditation. Just remember to blow it out once you are done. You can record this script and listen to it so you can close your eyes, or you can simply keep your eyes open and read through the words. Either way, you will connect with energy and it will benefit you.

Do what is most comfortable for you.

Let us begin.

Go ahead and get comfortable. Allow yourself to relax in a comfy chair or lie down if you feel inclined. Just know you won't be going to sleep during this meditation, as your consciousness will be focused and aware of everything you are doing and the energy that you are aligning to. Once you are comfortable, focus on your breathing. Feel the air as it hits the back of your throat, makes its way into your lungs, and fills your abdomen. As you exhale, feel the breath as it leaves your mouth. As you continue to breathe, bring a problem or situation you have been struggling with or a question for which you have been seeking an answer to the forefront of your mind. If there isn't real struggle in your life right now, perhaps you just wish to see what is being hidden from your current point of view. Either way, you will be intentionally meditating for something to be revealed that has been eluding you or that needs to be brought forward at this time.

Focus on the breath, inhaling through the nose and exhaling through the mouth. Get the breath to go as long and deep as possible. As you inhale, breathe in the question or situation. As you exhale, open yourself up to receive an answer or solution. Breathe in the unknown and breathe out that which is being revealed. As you get comfortable with the breath work, invite Archangel Raziel into your meditation space and into your energy and aura. Allow him to align you to the frequency of the known, the found, and the revealed. You may see him as a color or a beam of light, wrapping himself around your question, situation, or problem. He may also just appear in full form, ready to point out answers and speak unknown things to you. Just allow whatever is taking place to unfold, and stay with the breath work, inhaling deeply and slowly and exhaling fully. Stay with this energy until you feel that you have received all that is currently available to you. You will know when this happens, as you will feel a drop of energy or a coolness wash over you, or will have that inner knowing that your time is done.

Once you're complete and you know for sure your connection to what you seek has been released, slowly ground yourself back into your body and bring your awareness back to the room. While the experience is still fresh in your mind, grab your journal or a notepad and write down anything and everything that revealed itself to you, including how Raziel presented himself to you. If you have your answer or solution, your next step is to take action on it. However, if you feel that the information you received is incomplete, repeat the meditation until you have the answers you seek. Archangel Raziel never gets tired of answering questions, solving complex or simple problems, or even just showing you new things. So you can do this meditation over and over and over again.

Setting Up an Altar to 777 and Archangel Raziel

We all have things we want to learn. We all have new ideas, new skills, or new adventures we would like to explore. The first step to all of this newness is to be open to new knowledge, new wisdom, and new ways of being and doing. It is easiest to set this altar up to one new thing at a time. If you wish to go back to school, write a letter to yourself as if you are the admissions officer of the college or university you wish to attend. Tell yourself you have been accepted. Make it as lovely and full of wonder as you can dream of. If you are working toward a new job, write a letter from the personnel officer congratulating you on your new position. Whatever this new adventure is, write up a letter that gives you the green light. Claim it. Own it. Then place it on your altar along with an image or pictures that go along with what it is that you are asking Raziel to align for you. Things you will need for your altar include a picture of Archangel Raziel or an oracle card or printed-out picture with his image on it, a dark blue candle for open communication, 777 written on a green piece of paper, some salt for protection, a pinch of dirt to ground your prayer, some feathers to represent the angels, and anything else you feel you want to place upon the altar. You may also want to sit down and compose a prayer or intention statement to Raziel and 777. Here is an example of what you might say: "Raziel, I call on you to assist me to level up so that I can attain new skills and push myself in ways that cause me to grow and expand. I ask that you guide me and support me as I take a leap of faith into this unknown adventure."

Once you have your altar set up, I recommend cleansing it with an essential oil spray just to mentally and energetically clear the space and set it up for your prayer work. Once you have your magical tools and your altar is prepped, dressed, and ready to go, take a couple of deep breaths, light your candle, and speak your intention statement out loud, beginning with the words: "I call on Archangel Raziel and the power of 777 to hear my intention and assist me in achieving it in the smartest and wisest way possible. May my intention be for my higher good, as well as the good of all those who may be involved in bringing my intention into reality." Then go ahead and read your intention statement/prayer: "My intention/prayer is…"

To end the ritual, you can either blow the candle out or leave it burning if it is safe to do so. If you choose to blow your candle out, repeat these words first: "As I blow this candle out, I trust that its smoke carries my intention up to the heavens to be manifested by the Universe. I am ready to receive my asking, and so it is." Now, blow out your candle.

Your job now is to stay open and be receptive, trusting that Raziel has heard your prayer and that you have cast ripples into your future timeline.

Automatic Writing Prompts

After you have done your prayer work, or even after you have done the visualization, you will notice that your connection to Raziel is open and he is starting to communicate with you. This may come in the form of single words, sentences, or even just an inner knowing. If you feel moved to, think about pulling out your journal and capitalizing on this connection. Title your page "Talks with Raziel and the Vibrational Energy Known as 777." If you are familiar with journaling work, go ahead and start writing, as you will know how to feel the nudges of the information as it flows from the number 777 and Archangel Raziel. If you are new to journal work, consider using the writing prompts below to get you started with the process:

1. Raziel, how will I know when you are around?

2. Where am I not trusting myself and my inner wisdom?

3. Why have I struggled in the past to trust the unknown and step into my own inner wisdom?

4. How can I become more aware of Raziel's signs and trust that they are pointing me in the right direction?

5. How will stepping into the energy of 777 assist me today?

You may find that the prompts themselves get you into a nice writing flow, and before you know it, you have moved beyond them. Just lean into the process, trust that Raziel is guiding your hand, and do not try to make logical sense of anything that comes up initially.

Angel Crystal: Herkimer Diamond

The Herkimer diamond is one of the few crystals that you can use to store information and use it for later. They are like living notebooks. This makes them crystals of wisdom and keepers of knowledge. Hold on to one and it might just teach you something new even if it hasn't been charged. This makes this crystal the perfect stone to download and store the energy of 777 and Archangel Raziel. To code this crystal with the frequency of 777 and embed the energy of Archangel Raziel, first you will need to cleanse your Herkimer pocket stone. You can do this by passing it through the smoke of some burning sage, palo santo, or even cypress. You can also place it next to a salt lamp or onto a salt brick. You do this because you want your crystal notebook to be a blank canvas for your coding. You will also need to know when the next crescent moon is, as you will be harnessing the power of that particular moon phase. The crescent moon is when things are being brought out of the dark and into the light, much the way Raziel brings unknown things out of hiding.

Once you have prepped your crystal, you can begin to gather the rest of your magical tools. You will need a piece of paper, a pen, tape or a rubber band, some salt for protection (any salt will do), some dirt for grounding (any dirt is fine), some sugar to sweeten the spell (any sugar is fine), and a white (it stands in for all colors) or gold (to connect to the Divine) candle. A tea light will work if that is all you have on hand. Take your pinch of salt, sugar, and dirt and mix them up. This is for grounding and protecting the energy, all the while keeping the element of fun and play. Put the mixture in a small dish and place it to the side for the time being. Now, take your paper and write the number 777 on it as large as you possibly can, filling up the entire page. Next, place your Herkimer diamond in the middle of the paper and sprinkle your salt, sugar, dirt mixture over the top. Wrap your crystal up inside the paper and secure it with some tape or a rubber band. Place your Herkimer diamond bundle onto your altar. It can be the one you made specifically for your Raziel altar or one from any other altar you have set up for spellwork.

Make sure you are on the first night of the crescent moon phase and light your candle.

Repeat the following incantation:

> *I call on the power of 777 to activate my crystal.*
>
> *Give it the power to show me what has been hidden when the time is needed.*
>
> *I call in Archangel Raziel to infuse this crystal with his power*
>
> *to guide me to all the things I need to know, when I need to know them.*
>
> *I call the energy of the crescent moon to guide me out of the darkness of ignorance and into*
>
> *the light of knowledge and understanding.*
>
> *With these three energies combined, I now activate my crystal.*
>
> *As it is said, now it is done.*

Leave your Herkimer diamond on your altar until the first day of the full moon. Then unwrap it. Give the salt, sugar, and dirt mix back to the earth and place your crystal next to your bed or your workspace. Use it during meditation when you want to get an answer to a question or place it under your pillow to receive dreams that can bring you information and inspiration.

Additional Numbers for Working with Raziel's Energy

770—It's time to launch into something you have never done before. New things are a great way to learn, grow, and expand. Right now, your possibilities are endless.

771—Today is the day to learn something new about yourself. Give yourself a chance, take yourself out, and get to know yourself deeper than before.

772—Find out something new about your partner or spouse today. Ask them to share something you did not know about them.

773—Friends have a lot to teach us. Be on the lookout today for a friendly lesson on how to enjoy the world around you.

774—Structure doesn't always mean boring; in fact, oftentimes there are opportunities of expansion to be found in the most mundane of daily tasks.

775—Change is the best time to find a new skill, learn a new lesson, and expand your knowledge. Now is the time to harness the change in your life and see what knowledge it brings your way.

776—Caring for the self is a lifelong journey, one that has many twists and turns and one in which we constantly learn things about ourselves, our needs, and our desires. Today, use your self-care time to learn about a new desire you have.

778—The physical world is the greatest classroom there is. If you need an answer to a problem, then look around you, as it is more than likely right in front of your face.

779—Endings are points of growth and expansion; they teach us how to let go, how to be grateful, and how to leave things behind we no longer need. Today, an ending is offering you the space to let go and to learn how to be grateful for the endings you are currently experiencing.

9

888 ~ ARCHANGEL RAGUEL
You Are Currently in the
Flow of Divine Abundance

"Stay in divine flow and understand
the law of abundance in the physical
world starts with you."

Deeper Meaning of 888

The angel number 888 is here to remind you that you are always connected to divine flow. It may not always feel like it, but that is only because you aren't focused on what is going your way and are instead focused on what is not going the way you would like. Archangel Raguel and 888 want to bring you back to the flow. They want you to shift your point of perspective and start creating a vortex of flow. For when you are in alignment with flow, there always seems to be enough and you can't help but find even more areas of your life that are abundant. This is really how the law of abundance works. First, you start to find it, then you add to it, and before you know it you have created a giant magnet that just keeps attracting it.

When 888 shows up in your daily life, it is time to let flow happen, hand over your expectations and excuses to Raguel, and let him hold you in the river of divine abundance. Allow 888 to take you downstream to all that is waiting for you and to all that has always been waiting for you. Flow is that wonderful state in which everything just falls into place without effort. People, places, and situations line up for you with ease and grace. It is almost as if you are in the middle of an unfolding miracle. The angel number 888 is the frequency of this energy. It is the passcode to your personal divine abundance. However, to really step into this frequency, to learn how to impress it into your vibration, you first have to be aware of it. Archangel Raguel knows just how easy it can be to allow the outside world to dictate your flow and to let it contract you, even when there is no reason for it to do so. It is not surprising that some people constantly feel shut off, left out, or left behind. The angel number 888 tells us that it does not have to be this way and that you can look for evidence outside of yourself to support any point of view.

This is where the internal magic of 888 happens. The moment you decide, the second you choose to open the doors to divine abundance inside of you, you give the outside world permission to start lining up evidence to support you, which means the next time you see 888, connect with your inner self, allow it to show you how you are in the flow of divine abundance, visualize yourself being kissed by the Divine, and then let Archangel Raguel bring you the abundance that is rightfully yours. Start actively looking for things flowing into your life without effort. Open yourself up to receive with grace and watch as more love flows from you to all of those around you. This is how the divine law flows: from God, to you, to all those who come into your world. The angel number 888 says align, open, receive, share, repeat.

The Angel Raguel

Because I believe in transparency, I have to admit that Raguel is a pretty new angel to me, meaning we have not worked together that long. He is one of the many new angels that have just moved into my life in the last two years. In this respect, I see him as a bit of a leveling up angel. By this, I mean he comes along when you are ready to up level yourself and when you are getting ready to move into a new auric frequency. This really makes his connection to 888 even more powerful, as 8s really are about navigating the material world. To me, three 8s show the third level of managing the physical realm. At this level you have moved beyond base needs, have even shifted beyond ego wants and desires, and are now working to balance your spiritual needs and physical experience.

It is no mistake that Raguel, along with a handful of other angels, came into my life the moment I decided to let go of my current living experience. My wife and I decided that sitting still collecting more and more material things was not for us, so we gave everything away and put our lives into two suitcases. This pushed us to trust in divine flow, to have faith that our abundance would always be there and that the angels would not let us down. We stepped off the edge of the known and leapt without a safety net into the unknown. Waiting for us with open arms was Archangel Raguel. It was also not surprising that in the first couple of weeks of this new life we saw 888 everywhere, and I do mean everywhere, including hotel rooms, license plates, bank statements, and billboards. It was everywhere. In fact, every time I have a shaky moment, 888 will pop up, and I feel Raguel close by, reminding me to stay open, to look for the flow, to watch for the alignments, and to start collecting evidence that all is well and as it should be.

There is no doubt that when Archangel Raguel steps into your life, the trust you have in yourself gets an upgrade, for here, in the frequency of 888, you must have trust in yourself. You have to trust you will know when and where to align to the abundance flow. You also have to trust that you will know when and where to find proof that you have aligned with the law of abundance. You also have to trust that you will allow Archangel Raguel to bring you what you need, when you need it, every time, without exception. That's a lot of trust. This might explain why Raguel only shows up at certain times in one's life. You have to be ready for the energy he brings. You have to want to ride the frequency wave that 888 will bring you. And more importantly, you need to be willing to let go and trust.

Visualization/Meditation from Raguel:
Reset Your Core Feelings Around Abundance

In this guided meditation, you will be able to connect with Archangel Raguel and the vibrational energy of 888 to help bring more abundance into your life. There is no wrong or right way to journey through this meditation. You may feel sensations in your body, heat, cold, or even as if something or someone is touching your face and head as you move through the meditation script. You may even see colors, or your senses may become heightened. Also, you may feel nothing the first time you do this or maybe even the second or third. Just know that regardless of what does or does not happen to you, Raguel is there with you and will hold sacred space for you to explore all that will become visible to you. Make sure you do this meditation somewhere quiet where you will not be disturbed. If you feel called to, you can light a white candle, as this is an inclusive candle, and have it burning throughout the meditation. Just remember to blow it out once you are done. Feel free to record this script and listen to it so you can close your eyes, or you can simply keep your eyes open and read through the words.

Do what is most comfortable for you.

Before we begin this meditation, I want you to think of the three core feelings you wish to have an abundance of in your life. These three core feelings will create the vortex of energy of both your inner and outer world, so choose carefully which core feelings you wish to expand upon. Perhaps you would like to have an abundance of love, an abundance of kindness, or an abundance of peace. These are your feelings, and you get to choose which ones you want to use. Once you know what your three core feelings are going to be for this meditation, I recommend writing them down on a piece of paper so that you can have them with you.

Now, let us call in Archangel Raguel and ask him to stand with you today, to come forth and open your heart chakra, your third eye chakra, and your sacral chakra since you will be using these three energy centers to create, feel, and hold the vision of the expansive abundant energy you are to going call into your life today. Focus on your breath, breathing in through the nose and out through the mouth as deeply and slowly as you possibly can, trusting that as you relax your body, calm your mind, and focus on the breath, Archangel Raguel is slowly opening up your three chakras and infusing them with his angelic energy. As he continues to do this energy work on you, shift the focus of your mind to your second chakra, which is the space between your pelvis and is your center of creation. As you shift your focus to this energy center, send the feeling that you would like an abundance of to it. See the word moving into the light that Archangel Raguel has created and into your chakra. Take a deep breath, and then go ahead and send your second core feeling into that chakra as well. Next, go ahead and send the third one there so that all three core feelings are now being lovingly coded into your second chakra.

As you breathe, you will see that Archangel Raguel has given each of your core feelings—the energies that you wish to expand upon and have an abundance of in your life—a specific color. This color is a beautiful light that is swirling inside the second chakra. As you continue to inhale and exhale, watch as Archangel Raguel pulls this blended light up from the second chakra and places it inside your heart chakra. Now, you have connecting energy from your sacral to your heart as these three core feelings start to deepen their connection with both your physical and energetic body. Keep breathing and focusing on that light as it starts to move up your body even more. Take another slow, deep breath as Archangel Raguel moves these three bands of colorful light, these three core feelings, up into your third eye, the chakra in the middle of your forehead. He will be infusing this energy center, the center of vision and sight, with this colored energy. It is now that you'll be able to see what life will look like with an abundance of these energies pulsing through your body and expanding out into the world.

Imagine your day-to-day experience, blessed with an abundance of these three core feelings. See how you effortlessly move from one core feeling to another, wrapping it around your daily tasks and infusing everybody you come into contact with in this energy, literally changing the creation of your outside world. Continue to hold this vision as you see these beautiful lights, these three threads of color, expanding beyond you and into everyone you come into contact with. See them expanding out further into your community, into your state, and into your country, expanding all the way across the globe. Continue to send out this light to the entire world, embedding, impressing, encoding, and instructing this energy to become amplified, magnified, and abundant to you and all who require it. Stay with that vision for a couple of minutes, remembering to breathe slowly and deeply in through the nose and out through the mouth. When you feel the energy start to fade, take another nice deep breath and let go of that vision as Archangel Raguel finishes up his energy work, sending that light all the way through you, into every cell of your body.

When the vision has completely faded, go ahead and thank Archangel Raguel for showing up today and assisting you with this work. Return to the breath work, breathing in through the nose and out through the mouth as you slowly bring yourself back to center. Bring yourself back to the moment. Wiggle your toes and fingers and roll out your neck and shoulders as you gently bring your awareness back to your body and back to the room you are sitting in. When you are ready, open your eyes and get on with the rest of your day. If you did this meditation at night, drink some water to flush any toxins out of your kidneys and gently relax into slumber.

Setting Up an Altar to 888
and Archangel Raguel

This is your law of attraction altar. This is the one altar you can set up and leave up somewhere in your house and just keep changing out the things you wish to attract. This is the one altar you can also have the most fun with. Want Archangel Raguel to help you manifest a new car? Buy a toy car replica of the car you want and place it on your altar or find a picture of it online, print it out, and put that on your altar. Want to manifest more money? Buy a figurine of a bag of money or a pot of gold, or if you have images of money, you can use those as well. Want to manifest your dream vacation? Well, I think you know what you need to do. Go ahead and gather all your manifestation avatars and have fun getting your altar ready. Other things you will need for your blessings altar include a picture of Raguel or an oracle card with an image of him on it, a green or gold candle (as these colors are connected to abundance), 888 written on a gold or yellow piece of paper, some salt for protection, a pinch of dirt to ground the energy, some feathers to represent the angels, and anything else you feel you want to place upon the altar. You may also want to sit down and compose a prayer or intention statement to Raguel and 888.

An example might be as follows: "Raguel, keep me in the flow of my divine abundance. Show me how to keep my thoughts aligned to my vision. Assist me in setting my emotions on a positive outcome and allow me to bring more peace and grace into my daily life."

Once you have your altar set up, I recommend spraying it with a sage spray or giving it a once-over with sage or palo santo smoke just to mentally and energetically clear the space and fully set it up for your prayer work. Once you have dressed your altar and cleared your space, it is time to begin. Take a couple of nice deep breaths, light your candle, and speak your intention statement out loud, beginning with the words: "I call on Archangel Raguel and the power of 888 to hear my intention and assist me in achieving it in the most abundant way. May my intention be for my higher good and the good of all those who may be involved." Then go ahead and read your intention statement/ prayer: "My intention/prayer is ..."

To end the ritual, you can either blow the candle out or leave it burning if it is safe to do so. If you choose to blow your candle out, repeat these words first: "As I blow this candle out, I trust that its smoke carries my intention up to the heavens to be manifested by the Universe. I am ready to receive my asking, and so it is." Now, blow out your candle.

Your job now is to stay open, be receptive, and trust that all you are manifesting is on its way and will be arriving in divine time in the most divine way.

Automatic Writing Prompts

After you have done your prayer work, or even after you have done the visualization, you may notice your connection to Archangel Raguel will feel like it is open, and you may even find messages and information starting to trickle or flow through you. These may come in the form of single words, sentences, or even just an inner knowing. If you feel like you want to tap into this connection while it is open and flowing, think about pulling out your journal and capitalizing on this dialogue. Title your page "Talks with Raguel and the Vibrational Energy Known as 888." If you are familiar to journaling work, go ahead and start writing, as you will know how to feel the nudges of the information as it flows from the number 888 and Archangel Raguel. If you are new to journal work, consider using the writing prompts below to get you started with the process:

1. Raguel, how will I know when you are around?
2. Where am I not allowing flow into my life?
3. Why have I struggled in the past with the law of abundance and all the blessings it can bring into my everyday life?
4. How can I become more aware of the abundance in my life?
5. How will stepping into the energy of 888 assist me today?

You may find that the prompts themselves get you into a nice writing flow, and before you know it, you have moved beyond them. Just lean into the process, trust that Raguel is guiding your hand, and do not try to make logical sense of anything that comes up initially.

Angel Crystal: Carnelian

Carnelian is used to motivate, open up our creativity, and bring us into a deeper state of self-trust and self-worth. This makes it a fantastic stone to work with when we need to bring things we desire from the world of imagination into the physical world. It moves us into a state of trust, allowance, and acceptance. This is the "allow" and "receive" part of the ask-and-it-is-given equation. This makes carnelian the perfect stone to code with 888 and Archangel Raguel's energy. Seeding this crystal with the energy of 888 will make it a powerful manifesting crystal.

You will need the following magical supplies: a pocket stone or piece of carnelian, a piece of paper large enough to wrap your crystal in, a pen, some dirt, some salt, and some string. Once you have all your magical supplies gathered, grab your piece of paper and write 888 as many times as you can all over the page. Fill it up as much as possible. Once you have filled your paper up with 888, sprinkle your dirt and salt over the paper. Just a small sprinkling is all we are looking for. Now, place your crystal in the middle of the paper, wrap it up, and tie it all together with your string.

Pick up your little parcel with your right hand and place it next to your heart while placing your left hand over your sacral chakra. Take a slow, deep breath and allow yourself to settle. Drop your shoulders and let your neck get loose as you take another slow, deep breath. Feel yourself connecting to the energy from your sacral chakra, your heart chakra, and your crystal. With each inhale, feel the energy of the crystal and 888 being drawn into your heart. As you exhale, feel the creative energy open and expand out of your sacral chakra. Hold this energy via the breath work for as long as you can, slowly increasing your awareness of the presence of Archangel Raguel with you in the room. Just keep breathing. Keep inhaling the energy of the crystal, connecting it to the beat of your heart. Give yourself permission to fall even deeper into the energy of Raguel and exhale the expansive energy from the second chakra. When you feel done or you feel the current of energy has stopped running, stop the breath work and remove your hands from your body. You can go and place your little parcel on your altar to Archangel Raguel for the next twenty-four hours to deepen the energy, or if you feel your crystal is charged enough, open your parcel, place the salt and dirt back in the garden under a tree, and throw your paper and string in the recycling. You can now carry your carnelian with you or place it next to your work desk. I like to keep my manifesting crystals next to my workspace, as I personally feel they keep the space charged and open for creative flow. But you do you, boo!

Additional Numbers for Working with Raguel's Energy

880—Put your faith in the unknown, as the frequency of abundance relies on it to create miracles.

881—Now is the time to hold onto your vision, to keep walking the path and to not look over your shoulder. Leaders forge ahead regardless of whether there are people following them or not.

882—The inner world creates the outer world. If you wish to see more divine flow in your outside world, you must first connect to the divine flow inside you.

883—Abundance is a team sport. You cannot ride the flow of this frequency without cocreating with others. Today, take a moment to say thank you to all those who play a part in your abundant life.

884—The physical world does better when it is allowed to flow. Look for places in your life where you may have pinched off the flow and get the Divine moving in every corner of your experience.

885—Thank Archangel Raguel for change. Without it, life would never be able to get happier, healthier, or more joyfully delicious.

886—Abundance needs to be nurtured, just like other energy. How you feed it, talk to it, and engage with it dictates how it shows up in your world.

887—Knowing where abundance comes from and goes in your life will show you how you prioritize your flow. Knowledge is a powerful currency; claim it.

889—Abundance is a cycle; it ebbs and flows following the needs, wants, and desires of your vibrational frequency. You ask for something, it is sent, you trust and let go, then you receive. Find out where you are today in the cycle.

999 ~ ARCHANGEL RAPHIEL
Healing Energy Is
Around You

"You are currently in the frequency of
healing energy. Just relax, breathe,
and allow the healing to wash over you."

Deeper Meaning of 999

I have been working as an energy healer and coach for well over
a decade now, and one of the things that always surprises me is
how ill-informed a lot of people are about what healing is. Sure,
we know about physical healing: overcoming disease or even
recovering from an injury. However, healing work is so much
more involved and complex. We can be healing from trauma,
addiction, grief, pain, abuse, loneliness, abandonment, sadness,
depression, and so many other things. The list of what you could

be "healing" is so long, it would take days to run through it. This is why when you see 999, do not try to figure out what it is you may be healing from because you are more than likely wrong. Very rarely do we have an idea of what sort of healing work we need, as we tend to focus on where we feel the pain. But the pain is not the cause; it is a symptom. However, Archangel Raphiel knows, and he can send it right to the area you need it most.

You do not need to know, question, or figure it out; all you have to do is allow it in and remain open and receptive to the energy. The angel number 999 could offer healing in one part of your life today, then work on another aspect of you tomorrow. In this respect, 999 and Archangel Raphiel remind us that we are constantly in the flow of healing energy. There isn't a time when it is not flowing to us, through us, and around us. Sometimes it is working on your mind, other times your emotions, and other times your body. It could even be working on your aura, your chakras, or any part of your physical experience. Healing can take place anywhere and anytime. So, the next time you see 999, merely say, "I am open and ready to attune to the frequency of healing" or "Raphiel, I am open and receptive to your healing energy; heal me as you deem fit." Both of these statements open you up and drop your resistance to the flow of healing energy. The angel number 999 says, "Just drop your resistance and the healing can begin."

Allow yourself the freedom of not needing to figure it all out and just let 999 and Archangel Raphiel in to assist. There is something very liberating in letting go, dropping the need to be in control, and trusting yourself to a higher power. The angel number 999 is your reminder that you don't have to have things figured out and that sometimes it is actually wiser to surrender to an energy that knows better than your ego mind. The ego is the biggest obstacle to health and well-being. So, practice social distancing from your ego's influence and place yourself in the frequency of 999 and Archangel Raphiel instead. This is really how healing works in the body, mind, spirit, and vibration.

The Angel Raphiel

Raphiel is another one of those angels that doesn't seem to have a clear gender association, which is why I tend to refer to Raphiel as "they" or "them." Sometimes, they will show up in masculine form, sometimes in feminine, and sometimes in non-gendered form. It would appear fitting into a strict human structure is not this archangel's jam. It is also another reason you might find yourself spelling their name differently as well. When I was writing this book I kept changing between spellings. The spelling I finally decided on is the one that to me feels like the nonbinary version of this archangel. However, if Archangel Raphiel does appear or present to you in a specific gendered way, by all means continue working with them that way. Raphiel is more concerned with spreading healing and healing energy than anything else. Health, well-being, prosperity, and happiness are much more important to this archangel than what gendered form they choose to show up in.

Archangel Raphiel would rather you focus on the aspects of yourself or your life that need healing and allow them to fade into the background so the energy you require can be given completely and fully. This is being of true service, and I do believe there is a lesson for all of us in how Archangel Raphiel chooses to prioritize service over self-labeling. The work is more important than the identity. The "we" is more essential than the "me." The angel number 999, along with Archangel Raphiel, are here to assist in showing you how to be of service in a spiritual way. This is a lesson in seeing how healing is connected to the whole and not the parts that make it up—in other words, the "we" not the "me." That which needs to be identified is only one part of the whole, which is why it is important to let healing energy flow where it needs to go and not direct it to where the ego thinks it needs to go.

Call on Archangel Raphiel to assist you in times of struggle or when you feel intense fear, anxiety, and panic. These sorts of emotions wreak havoc on one's immune system and are not aligned with health and well-being. Ask Archangel Raphiel to heal your mind, calm your emotions, and bring you back to a state of peace and grace. Let Archangel Raphiel and the number 999 bring you back into the vortex of healing and attune you to the frequencies your body, mind, spirit, and life need right now in this moment. Healing changes moment to moment, which is why you want to stay grounded into the now, not in the past or the future. Archangel Raphiel will never heal you from a place in the past, meaning you can't go back and heal what has already been done. Raphiel will also never future-cast your healing energy. By this I mean they will not tell you what your health will or will not be in the future, as all healing will be done right here, right now. It is in the present moment that the past is healed and the healing energy is set for the future self. This means what happens now ripples through to the past as healing energy and toward the future to create a healed experience. So, the next time you see 999, just know Archangel Raphiel is right there with you and healing is taking place, healing that will not only benefit you but all those around you.

Visualization/Meditation from Raphiel: Receive Healing from the Angels

In this guided meditation you are going to connect to the healing energy of Archangel Raphiel and the vibrational energy of 999. This is a self-healing meditation and there is no wrong or right way to journey through it. You may experience physical sensations during this meditation or emotional waves, or you may not experience anything at all. Just know that regardless of what does or does not happen to you, Raphiel is there with you and will hold sacred space for you to explore. Make sure you do this meditation somewhere quiet where you will not be disturbed. If you feel called to, you can light a green candle for health and healing and have it burning throughout the meditation. If you cannot find a green candle, a white tea light will do just fine. Just remember to blow it out once you are done. You can record this script and listen to it so you can close your eyes, or you can simply keep your eyes open and read through the words. Either way, you will connect with energy and it will benefit you.

Do what is most comfortable for you.

Before we begin this meditation, think about an area of your life that you want to send healing energy to. Bring this area of your life to the forefront of your mind. Perhaps it is your health, perhaps it's a relationship, perhaps it's your job or career. You could even ask for healing around any resistance you may have about taking action on your next step or a new project. You don't need to know exactly where the healing will be directed, just the general area you would like Archangel Raphiel to direct the energy to. Leave the specifics to Raphiel.

Once you have identified the area in your life that you would like to send this healing to, go ahead and ask Archangel Raphiel to move into your energy field and into your auric body. You can do this by simply saying, "Archangel Raphiel, I call upon you to help heal and reset my vibrational body and cleanse my auric field." Once you have called Raphiel forward, go ahead and get comfortable. Put some music on if you feel inclined and take a long, slow, deep breath. Focusing on your breath work as you bring your mind in alignment with your body in the present moment, breathing deeply in through the nose and out through the mouth as you focus on relaxation, calm, and peace. The more relaxed you can be, the more healing energy your vibrational body can absorb. As you begin to relax your shoulders, drop the stress in your neck, feel the pressure of the day drop from your body, and breathe deeper. Trust that Raphiel is pumping healing energy into the area of your life for which you have requested their assistance. Your job is simply to relax and allow the energy to flow where it needs to go, trusting that this angelic healing is taking place, will continue to take place, and is available to you upon asking at any time. You may even see Archangel Raphiel's energy as a colored light, wrapping around and infusing itself into your chosen life area, but if you don't, that is fine. Healing energy is being sent either way.

You can stay in this state and focus on the breath work for as long as you feel is necessary. It may be a couple of minutes or it may be half an hour. Trust your intuition and know that when your session with Archangel Raphiel is complete, you will notice a shift in the energy around you. You might all of a sudden notice you feel warm or cold air on your face or body. You may feel a breath of air over your face or you might even feel some-body playing with your hair. This is an indication that your ses-

CLEAR QUARTZ

TIGER'S-EYE

AMETRINE

RUBY

JADE

SUNSTONE

ROSE QUARTZ

HERKIMER DIAMOND

CARNELIAN

PREHNITE

KYANITE

MOONSTONE

LARIMAR

sion is over. When you get this physical sensation, slowly bring yourself back to center, opening your eyes, scanning the room, rolling out your neck, and stretching your hands, fingers, and toes. Take nice, slow breaths as you bring your awareness back to your day and back to the tasks ahead. When you're ready, you can get up from your relaxed position and get on with the rest of your daily activities.

Setting Up an Altar to 999 and Archangel Raphiel

Your healing altar will be different from your other altars. This altar is strictly dedicated to your health and well-being. This is an altar you can keep up for as long as you want. You don't have to wait until you feel out of alignment with health to use this altar. In fact, I highly recommend you set this altar up when you are feeling as healthy as possible. If, however, you do suffer from chronic illness, do this when your mind can focus on health and well-being. Your body may not be where you want it to be, but you can always get your mind pointed in the direction of wellness. The reason you want to do it when your mind can focus on health and well-being is you want to have as many well-being vibes as possible surrounding your altar. Set this altar up when you feel as good as you can, whatever that may mean for you! Place items on this altar that represent how you feel when you are doing well. This might be pictures of you hiking, camping, boating, or some other happy, healthy picture or pictures you want to place on this altar. Other things you will need for your blessings altar include a picture of Raphiel or an oracle card with his or her image on it or one you have printed out, a green candle, 999 written on a green piece of paper, some salt, a pinch of dirt, some feathers, and anything else you feel you want to place upon the altar. You may also want to sit down and compose a prayer or intention statement to Raphiel and 999. An example might be the following: "Raphiel, I am ready to bask in the vibrations of my divine health. I am open to being in a state of constant well-being. I am relying on you to remind me that health and well-being are always there for me and they never have to be limited or in short supply."

Once you have your altar set up, cleanse it by visualizing a white light exploding over it, like a white bomb exploding and clearing out any and all unwanted energy. This will set up your altar for your prayer work. Then, take a couple of nice deep breaths, light your candle, and speak your intention statement out loud, beginning with the words: "I call on Archangel Raphiel and the power of 999 to hear my intention and to assist me in achieving it in the most healing way possible. May my intention be for my higher good, as well as the good of all those who may be involved in bringing it into reality." Then go ahead and read your intention statement/prayer: "My intention/prayer is ..."

To end the ritual, you can either blow the candle out or leave it burning if it is safe to do so. If you choose to blow your candle out, repeat these words first: "As I blow this candle out, I trust that its smoke carries my intention up to the heavens to be manifested by the Universe. I am ready to receive my asking, and so it is." Now, blow out your candle.

Automatic Writing Prompts

After you have done your healing work, you may notice that your connection to Raphiel is more open than usual. This might mean that messages and information may start to trickle or flow through to your conscious mind. These messages might come in the form of single words, sentences, or even just an inner knowing. If you feel moved to, think about pulling out your journal and capitalizing on this connection. Title your page "Talks with Raphiel and the Vibrational Energy Known as 999." If you are familiar with journaling work, go ahead and start writing, as you will know how to feel the nudges of the information as it flows from the number 999 and Archangel Raphiel. If you are new to journal work, consider using the writing prompts below to get you started with the process:

1. Raphiel, how will I know when you are around?
2. Where am I not allowing healing and well-being into my life?
3. Where have I struggled in the past to connect with the healing energy of Raphiel in my everyday life?
4. How can I become more aware of your healing energy in my career?
5. How will stepping into the energy of 999 assist me today?

You may find that the prompts themselves get you into a nice writing flow, and before you know it, you have moved beyond them. Just lean into the process, trust that Raphiel is guiding your hand, and do not try to make logical sense of anything that comes up initially.

Angel Crystal: Prehnite

This crystal is often given to healers, as it is known as the "heal the healers" stone. It is a heart chakra stone that works on opening the heart and using it as a powerful healing tool. That is what makes it the perfect stone to code in and set with the frequencies of 999 and Archangel Raphiel. Magical tools you will need for this exercise include a pocket-size prehnite, a piece of paper, a red pen, a green candle for healing energy, a piece of string or tape, and a picture of Raphiel. This exercise is to create a crystal that resonates with the healing frequencies of 999. Please note this is just a talisman, an object to help keep your mind focused on all the healing energy coming into your life. This crystal will not cure you of an illness, and it does not take the place of a doctor or medical treatment.

Once you have gathered your magical tools, get your piece of paper and your red pen and draw a large heart on the paper, one that takes up as much of the paper as possible. Around the edge of the heart, write the numbers 999 as many times as it takes to go all the way around the outline of the heart. In the middle of your heart, place your picture of Archangel Raphiel. Then, on top of the picture, place your pocket-size prehnite. Now, wrap your crystal up in the paper and seal it with either a small piece of tape or by tying it up with your piece of string. Take your small package to your Raphiel altar. You may wish to add other items to your altar at this time. If you have a health and well-being vision board, you might want to add that as well, but you don't have to. Once you have your altar set up, go ahead and light your green candle and say the following prayer:

> *Archangel Raphiel, I call unto you.*
> *Infuse this crystal with the healing energy of your heart.*
> *Fill it with the frequency of 999,*
> *and recode it to assist me in maintaining my health and well-being goals.*
> *As it is said, so it is done.*

Now, leave your little crystal package on your altar until your candle burns down. If you are unable to let your candle burn down and have to blow it out, leave your crystal on the altar and do the prayer again until you have completely burned down your candle. Once you are done, unwrap your crystal and use it when you feel the need to bring Archangel Raphiel and the energy of 999 into your day. You can repurpose the image of Raphiel and the paper with your heart on it and use them for your Raphiel altar or use them with your health and well-being vision board. If not, please find a responsible way to dispose of them.

Additional Numbers for Working with Raphiel's Energy

990—There are unlimited ways to channel healing energy into your life right now, so just let go and let it flow.

991—There is something very personal and internal that needs you to allow healing energy to flow into it. Don't deny it; own it and allow Archangel Raphiel to bring the healing to your internal world.

992—Healing is flowing through your heart-connected relationships today, so open your heart and let the healing energy flow from your heart to someone you love.

993—There is a social space that you frequent that needs you to send some healing energy its way. Ask people today how they are doing and let them know you honor them.

994—Fear is just another opportunity to heal. Wherever you feel fear today, surrender it to Archangel Raphiel for healing.

995—Change is just another word for healing. When we heal the past, we simultaneously send healing energy to the future. And we do it all by making change in the present moment.

996—It is time to cleanse your home. Clear out all the old energy and reset it with new healing frequencies of love, joy, and well-being.

997—Today, take some time off and rest, as this is one of the most healing things you can do for your body, mind, and soul.

998—Everything in your world needs healing, not because it is broken but because it deserves love, compassion, and acknowledgment.

11

1010 ~ ARCHANGEL GABRIEL
You Are One
with Everything

"Learn the law of wholeness and understand
your place in the universal matrix."

Deeper Meaning of 1010

Many people, especially those who are walking a healing path, have felt that they are not enough, that they lack something, or that others have something they themselves will never be able to attain. Comparison is separation from Source energy. Lack is separation from your own divine self. Allowing the mind to question your inner knowing causes you to disconnect from Source energy and unplugs you from the feeling of being complete and whole. The angel number 1010 is your reminder that you are not separate. Archangel Gabriel says to think of connection like a train ride. Sometimes there are seats on the train and you get to have a little more comfort on your commute. Other times, you have to hang onto a railing or some other sort of strap. These can be difficult to hold, and you often find yourself unable to grip them and sometimes let go completely. At that point, you can feel unsupported and at the mercy of the movement of the train. Your level of safety and stability end up on high alert, and you feel alone as you are flung about by the rocking and thrusting of the train we are calling life. However, 1010 reminds you that you can always grab back onto the strap to Source. You can reconnect with the energy that made you and find an available seat.

Sometimes this disconnection is temporary, and sometimes it seems like it is your whole life. The truth is, the rail, the hand grip, and the support are always there. You just have to want to reach up and grab hold. The seats are also always there. The people who managed to get a seat aren't luckier than you are; they just don't question their connection. They believe they will be supported and therefore are. They are tuned in to the frequency of 1010 and trust Archangel Gabriel to be there to provide for them. The difference is belief. The angel number 1010 wants you to reach up, to believe in your place in the universal matrix, to see yourself being whole and supported, and to see yourself sharing the ride with everyone else on the train. The angel number 1010 wants you to do this with the understanding that you all want the same thing, and that is to get to your destination happy and unharmed. The question of getting to your destination whole is never in doubt because you always will. When you see 1010, just take a moment and reach up and grab for the rail. Feel the energy of Archangel Gabriel flow through you as you curl your fingers together and form a fist around the hand of the Divine. Take a long, slow, deep breath and allow yourself to feel whole, complete, and at one with the energy that created you. When you feel stable and safe, let go and bring your arm back down, trusting that once you have made the connection, you do not need to make it again unless you really feel lost, alone, and at the mercy of the ride we call life.

The Angel Gabriel

Archangel Gabriel always comes to me in their feminine form, but that may not be how she shows up for you. Gabriel, or Gabbie as I often call her, tends to show up when she is attached to one of my clients. Generally speaking, she is a healing angel and comes to assist or oversee a healing that is taking place in my clients. This could be anything from healing physical illness to healing loneliness, depression, money wounds, love—you name it, Gabbie is there to assist in the healing process. She does this through reconnection or rejoining. Gabbie explains our need for healing in this way: "When one feels they are separate, disconnected, or alone, they tear open a wound in their vibrational body. This can cause damage to the aura and the chakras. This wound then affects the mind and body as well. When one comes to be healed, really all we are doing is reminding them that they are not separate and that there is no such thing as you and them, or me and you. There is only us and we. Everything is one. It comes from the same energy and will go back to the same energy." (This was channeled from Archangel Gabriel.)

This is why 1010 works so well with her healing energy. The number 1 is that which comes from nothing, or more to the point, the ego, "I," that is born from the unlimited potential of everything. Without 0 there is no 1, and yet 1 cannot exist without first coming from nothing. This means everything outside of you came from you, including your body and your mind. You are both the 0 and the 1. Confused yet? Don't worry, you are not alone. Even though I know this, it still seems to play tricks with my head, but that is only because the ego, "I," likes to see itself as separate and as its own being, standing alone from the rest of creation. Yet, this is not true, as we are never alone or separate. Yet the mind loves to listen to the ego. It loves to believe that it has meaning and purpose that is separate from everyone else. I have seen the result of this line of thinking make its way to my healing table again and again over the last decade. The sadness, the confusion, the frustration, the anger, and the illness this line of thinking and living brings can be devastating.

The good news is this is not how it needs to be because this is not how it is, and Archangel Gabriel and 1010 are here to remind you that you are not alone. You are not separate. You and everything around you are one, sharing the same heart, the same dream, and the same vision of creation. Just because it may look different on the outside does not mean it vibrates differently. Visual contrast is not the same as vibrational contrast. No two people will share the same ideas about love, but that does not mean they do not both strive and crave the same frequency we call love. No two people will share the same idea of joy, but that does not mean they do not both vibrate the same joy frequency. Do you see where we are going with this? Of course you do. Archangel Gabriel is here to remind you that how you feel, what you dream, and what you crave is at the heart of all sentient beings. It may not look the same, but it is all vibrating to the same frequency. We are all one; different, but one. We all come from zero, and to zero we will return. We all come into physical form to live through the energy of the one, and we will all drop the one and the physical and return to zero. We are all on the same journey and the same path; we just choose to walk it to our own unique beat. When we can truly understand this, we will heal that separation wound and rejoice in our place in the universal matrix.

Visualization/Meditation from Gabriel: Connecting to Your Life

Make sure you do this meditation somewhere quiet where you will not be disturbed. If you feel called to, you can light an apple-green candle for healing the heart and have it burning throughout the meditation. Just remember to blow it out once you are done. You can record this script and listen to it so you can close your eyes, or you can simply keep your eyes open and read through the words. Either way, you will connect with energy and it will benefit you.

Do what is most comfortable for you.

Let us begin.

If you have decided to light a candle, go ahead and do so now. Next, get into a comfortable position sitting in a comfy chair or a yoga pose or even lying down. Just direct your mind to pay attention to the script and be alert to any and all visions you may experience during this meditation. Take a deep, slow breath in through the nose and out through the mouth. Again, slowly inhale deeply through the nose, feeling the breath as it hits the back of your throat and makes its way into your lungs. Exhale through an open mouth and feel the air as you push it out of your body. Focus this breath work, making it as rhythmic as you can with equal-length inhales and exhales, letting your body and breath find their own natural flow. As you continue the breath work, call in Archangel Gabriel. Ask them to come into your energy, to your inner vision, and into the room with you.

You may notice Gabriel as male, female, both, or even gender neutral. Just allow the Gabriels to show up in the form they feel is best for you, your healing, and this meditation. Even if you don't notice a figure or sense a presence with you in the room, do not worry. Gabriel is there supporting you, honoring you, and witnessing your request. Just relax and deepen the breath work as you let yourself be protected and held by Gabriel's energy. As you open to this act of receiving, let yourself sink deeper into the moment and open yourself up a little more, keeping the breath slow, deep, and rhythmic. Now, bring to the forefront of your mind the area of your life you are struggling to feel connected with. This should be an area of your life in which you feel alone and separate. Do your best not to make judgments as you move your focus to this area of your life. Just let it bubble up, and hold the vision or the "feeling" of it as best you can. Once you have the vision or feeling of this concern, allow Gabriel to show you where the connecting threads are.

Watch as they light up all of the threads that connect this area of your life to other people, places, or things. Just observe; do not try to guide the vision, image, or feeling. Instead, focus on your breath work, inhaling through the nose and exhaling through the mouth. Keep watching until all of the threads have been illuminated. See how this web connects you to the world around you. Really focus on the people and places these threads connect to, as these are the people who hold the space for you to feel whole, complete, and part of something bigger. Sink into the feeling you get as you see how connected and aligned you are. Notice the sensation as it moves through your body, and you realize you stand with many right here, right now, in this moment, all threaded together as one. Stay with this vision as long as you feel guided to. Let its energy wrap around you.

When you feel that connection kick back in and this part of your life feels part of you once again, take a breath, and as you exhale, blow all of the threads away. Watch as all of the lights go out. Notice that you no longer feel alone, separate, or disconnected because even though the threads are no longer illuminated, you know they are there. You know you are part of something larger than yourself. You know you are complete, aligned, and playing your part in the grander scheme of the Universe. Take a breath and release any lingering doubts you have about this area of your life. Take another breath and see Gabriel slowly begin to leave. Thank them as they fade away, knowing that just like the threads, the angels are there regardless of if you can see them or not. Focus back on your breath work as you slowly bring your focus back to your body and back to the room you are sitting in. When you feel alert and ready, open your eyes. If you are able to, keep the candle burning. If not, go ahead and blow it out and get on with your day.

Setting Up an Altar to 1010 and Archangel Gabriel

One of the hardest things for most of us to remember is that we are complete and whole, that we do not need to be fixed, and that we are perfect just the way we are. This is why, for this altar, you will be writing a letter to yourself reminding yourself of this very fact. You can start it by placing your name at the top, and if you don't think you are overly imaginative with writing, you can just add a line that says: "Here is a list of things to remind myself that I am whole, complete, and one in the eyes of the [Divine/Universe/God/Goddess]." You can list as many items as you want or even as few as three. The number isn't as important as the complete letter you will then place on your altar. Other things you will need for your altar include a picture of Gabriel or an oracle card with their image on it, a white candle to represent all becoming one, 1010 written on a white piece of paper, some salt, a pinch of dirt, some feathers, and anything else you feel you want to place upon the altar.

You may also want to sit down and compose a prayer or intention statement to Gabriel and 1010. An example might be: "Gabriel, when I falter, remind me of who I am. Whisper in my ear all the ways I am complete and whole. Remind me that I am not broken and I do not need to be fixed. I understand I am a glorious work in progress, just like the Universe itself, for I am made of stardust, which makes the Universe and me one, complete and whole."

Once you have your altar set up, I recommend spraying it with a sage spray or giving it a once-over with smoke from an herb bundle. This will energetically and mentally clear the space and set it up for your prayer work. Once you have gathered your magical tools, cleansed your altar, and have everything ready, take a couple of nice deep breaths, light your candle, and speak your intention statement out loud, beginning with the words: "I call on Archangel Gabriel and the power of 1010 to hear my intention, to assist me in achieving it in the most holistic way. May my intention be for my higher good and the good of all those who may be involved in bringing it into reality." Then go ahead and read your intention statement/prayer: "My intention/ prayer is..."

To end the ritual, you can either blow the candle out or leave it burning if it is safe to do so. If you choose to blow your candle out, repeat these words first: "As I blow this candle out, I trust that its smoke carries my intention up to the heavens to be manifested by the Universe. I am ready to receive my asking, and so it is." Next, blow out your candle.

Automatic Writing Prompts

Having now worked through the meditation and the prayer work, you may notice that your connection to Gabriel in their many forms is more open, and you may notice messages and information starting to trickle or flow on through your conscious mind. These may come in the form of single words, sentences, or even just an inner knowing. If you feel moved to, think about pulling out your journal and capitalizing on this connection. Title your page "Talks with Gabriel and the Vibrational Energy Known as 1010." If you are familiar with journaling, go ahead and start writing, as you will know how to feel the nudges of the information as it flows from the number 1010 and Archangel Gabriel. If you are new to journal work, consider using the writing prompts below to get you started with the process:

1. Gabriel, how will I know when you are around?

2. Where am I not allowing myself to feel more connected in my everyday life?

3. Why is connection easier with some of the people in my life and not others?

4. How can I become more aware of my place in my family, community, or workplace?

5. How will stepping into the energy of 1010 assist me today?

You may find that the prompts themselves get you into a nice writing flow, and before you know it, you have moved beyond them. Just lean into the process, trust that Gabriel is guiding your hand, and do not try to make logical sense of anything that comes up initially.

Angel Crystal: Kyanite

Kyanite is the go-to crystal for balance and alignment of the mental and spiritual bodies, which makes it the perfect stone to code and ground the energy of 1010. The angel number 1010 is about balance and finding harmony and wholeness in each and every moment, bringing together yin and yang energies. This is best done into a kyanite pendant, but it will also work for a pocket stone if you do not wish to wear the stone. Magical tools you will need for this exercise are a kyanite pendant or pocket stone, a pen, and some paper.

On your paper, write 1010 as large as you can. Place your kyanite onto it, and place both hands just above your stone. Your hands should not be touching the stone, but you may feel some warmth or some other sort of physical sensation as you code the energy into it. Take a couple of slow, deep breaths, and close your eyes if you feel inclined to. Imagine Gabriel's energy flowing out of your hands and into the stone. See this energy mixing with the numbers 1010 and infusing your stone. Keep breathing and holding your hands over your stone until you feel like you are complete. This might be when you notice the energy in your hands stops or your hands get cold, or you may feel a slight breeze blowing across your hands. Either way, you will know when it is time to stop. Trust your gut.

Once you are complete, you can fold the paper up and either place it on your altar to Gabriel or throw it away. Your pendant is ready to wear or your pocket stone is ready to be carried around with you. You may find you don't need to wear it all the time, just on days when you feel the need to reconnect or get balanced, or when you feel out of alignment. Your pendant or pocket stone will bring you back to center and back to wholeness.

Additional Numbers for Working with Gabriel's Energy

1011—A good leader knows that when everyone on the team feels valued and integral, the whole team sees success as a personal achievement.

1012—It is not that you come to others to feel whole, it is that when you are already in the frequency of wholeness, you are open to truly be one with others.

1013—Now is the time to think of "we" not "me," for when we see ourselves as everyone, we engage in the world with compassion and kindness.

1014—Structure, routine, and daily habits will make you feel balanced, grounded, and connected. The magic is in the mundane nature of repetition.

1015—When you know who you are, change is something you celebrate, as you understand that no matter what comes your way, you can handle it.

1016—Community is an extension of self. When you feel you are one with who you are, you will be able to assist your community to feel happy, healthy, and whole.

1017—Alignment is an inside job, so when you feel off-balance, take a moment to stop, look around, and count seven things you can see right now in front of you. This will keep you balanced and in the moment.

1018—Money likes to flow and to stay in balance, which means if you want to feel connected to the flow of abundance, do not cling to material things, but instead, see your material world as complete and whole.

1019—When a cycle is complete, it means you have come full circle. A full circle is whole. Right now something has come to an end, and a cycle is now complete and whole. It is done, and it is time to move on.

12

1111 ~ ARCHANGEL SANDALPHON

Make a Wish,
the Universe Is Listening

"You live in a friendly universe, and it wants
to make all of your wishes come true. So
make a wish, trust that it has been heard,
and know that it is on its way back to
you in the most perfect and divine way."

Deeper Meaning of 1111

Archangel Sandalphon wants you to understand that the Universe is truly conspiring for your highest and better good always, without exception. Regardless of what is going on in your life right now, when you see 1111, stop, clear your mind, and ask for the wish that is in your heart. Your heart is the key to your

wishes, not your head, so don't think, feel. Take a breath, connect, and wish. Archangel Sandalphon wants you to know that
what beats in your heart beats into the universe. It is the loudest
part of who you are, vibrationally speaking, and this is the part
of you that the friendly universe is always trying to align you
with. The angel number 1111 says, "Be brave, trust, and let that
wish go. Surrender it up to the angels and let them bless you.
Let the energy of 1111 bring you what is in your heart, and
allow yourself to receive it." Sandalphon knows that this may
seem easier said than done for some of you, especially when your
mind may be telling you something very different. Your mind
may allow you to wish, but it may do whatever it can to block
you from receiving. It might try and convince you that what
your heart wants is impossible or that you are not worthy of your
wish, or it may even try to convince you that your wish needs
some form of payment. None of this is true, none of it.

You ask. You receive. That is it. It is a simple two-step process, nothing more, nothing less. When you see 1111, place your
hand on your heart and make a wish. Inhale the energy of 1111
and exhale your wish right into the open hands of Archangel
Sandalphon. Allow him to take your wish and place it in the
hands of those who are ready and waiting to create it for you. I
bet you didn't even know there is a team of vibrational beings on
standby to grant you your wishes, but there is, and it is their job
to make your wishes come true, including the hopes and dreams
you keep in your heart, the wishes that beat within you, and the
wishes that only the angels can hear and you can feel.

So what's in your heart?

What does it wish for?

Give it a voice and allow it to beat as loudly as it needs to the
next time you see 1111. Beating, asking, releasing, giving life to

your wishes. They are simple, pure, and divine. Sandalphon says no wish is too big or too small. If it is in your heart, it is perfect in every way, and he is ready and waiting to hear the wish that beats deep in your heart.

The Angel Sandalphon

Archangel Sandalphon's origin story has similarities to Metatron's as he, too, once walked the earth as human and, given his earthly good deeds, was granted a divine role as the celestial postman. In this respect, he is said to deliver prayers and wishes from heaven and place them into God's inbox. There are even stories of Sandalphon being so huge that his feet were planted on earth and his head was in heaven. My personal experiences with this angel aren't quite a match with this image of a celestial giant, but I do admit, he is one fantastic postal worker. Sandalphon is always ready and willing to take your request to the higher realms and to be the communication bridge between the earth and that which many call heaven. In this respect, Sandalphon has a very specific role in the celestial workplace and can be linked to other communication deities like Mercury or Hermes who ironically had wings on their shoes. The idea of a celestial postal service is pretty damn cool, and it allows us to truly get into the vibrational energy of seeing our messages being picked up and delivered lovingly to whoever is in charge of helping us out.

The angel number 1111 in many respects is a reminder that the lines are open and now would be the ideal time to drop your request into the vortex. We all need reminders that we can ask for help. How often do you forget to ask or just open your mouth and really ask for what you want? Archangel Sandalphon knows that for many humans this is not something that comes naturally or easily. Yet, he is a reminder that we are expected to do this and that there is a whole team of celestial beings just waiting to take our request. The more you call on Sandalphon and work with 1111, the easier it will become to ask, let go, trust, and receive because at the end of the day, that is the order in which it happens. You see 1111, you send in your wish. You let it go lovingly into the hands of Archangel Sandalphon, and then you trust that he has delivered it to the appropriate heavenly department. Now, sit back and wait to receive your wish. What wishes do you want to give to Sandalphon?

Visualization/Meditation from Archangel Sandalphon: Make a Wish!

Wishes can cause us to contract, which seems strange to say. However, oftentimes we have so much resistance to what we want that it can contract our energy from even thinking about making a wish. During this meditation, you will call in Archangel Sandalphon to assist you in staying open when you wish while also allowing the energy of 1111 to ease and release any of the resistance you are holding in your energy field, mind, or body. There is no wrong or right way to experience the energy of the angels. You may feel sensations in your body, heat, cold, or even as if something or someone touches your face and head as you move through the meditation script. You might even see colors, or your senses may become heightened. You may feel nothing the first time you do this or maybe even the second or third. Just know that regardless of what does or does not happen to you, Sandalphon is there with you and will hold sacred space for you to explore whatever comes up during your time together. Make sure you do this meditation somewhere quiet where you will not be disturbed. If you feel called to, you can light a birthday candle and have it burning throughout the meditation, blowing it out once you are done, just like you would when making a wish over your birthday cake. In fact, if you want to bring in the element of play, put your candle into a cupcake and bring in the birthday vibes. The more playful and fun you can make this, the easier it will be to stay open and drop your resistance. You can record this script and listen to it so you can close your eyes, or you can simply keep your eyes open and read through the words. Either way, you will connect with energy and it will benefit you.

Do what is most comfortable for you.

Let us begin.

Go ahead and get comfortable either in a chair, on the floor, or on your bed. It doesn't matter where you do this visualization, as your mind will be alert and focused and fully engaged in this guided meditation practice. Focus on your breath as you take deep slow inhales through the nose and long expressive exhales through the mouth, making sure to extend the breath in both depth and length. Feel the breath as it comes in the nose and down the throat, and then feel it as it is pushed out through the mouth. With each breath, you become more calm and relaxed. As you get deeper into the breath work, notice the tension slowly releasing from your shoulders and neck. Feel your lower back loosen. Even feel the arches of your feet relax and soften. As you continue to breathe slowly and deeply, notice how your body enters into this beautiful state of relaxation and receptivity. As you go deeper and relax even more, call in Archangel Sandalphon and ask him to come and be with you in this space, right here, right now. You may instantly know when Sandalphon has entered your energy, or you may just have a knowing that Sandalphon is there, ready to assist you. Either way, just trust that Archangel Sandalphon is there to support you through this process.

Take another deep, slow breath, and relax even further. As you continue the breath work and stay in this receptive and relaxed energy, bring to mind something that you have been wishing for a really long time and something that you've tried to achieve more than once but it has not happened yet. As you bring this desire, this wish, to the forefront of your mind, allow yourself to feel all the emotions that come with it, including feelings of excitement for the wish, feelings of sadness or grief because it has yet to manifest, or feelings of defeat or even failure because no matter how many times you have tried, the wish has yet to be fulfilled. Just let them bubble up to the surface. As each of these feelings pop up, see them forming small glass balls. When the balls form completely, put them in your hands and give them to Archangel Sandalphon. Do your best not to judge these emotions as good or bad, and just see them forming into these beautiful glass balls and yourself handing them off to the angel, knowing that Sandalphon will take care of all of them.

Keep forming these glass balls until there are no emotionally charged feelings left around your wish. You should be able to think about your wish without feeling hooked or charged or triggered in any way. Once this happens, thank Archangel Sandalphon for coming and assisting you throughout this process. Once Archangel Sandalphon leaves your energy, take your fingers and place them onto your third eye and say, "I impress and instruct this wish into my mind with the power of 1111." Again, gently press the third eye with your fingertips and say, "I instruct and impress this wish into my mind with the power of 1111." Take a nice deep breath in through the nose and out through the mouth, allowing yourself to sway gently. Sway from side to side as you drop the last of your resistance, the last of that emotional dust off your shoulders and off your body. When you feel complete and confident that your wish is ready for you to finally fulfill it, take another deep long breath. Bring your focus back to your body and back to the room. Take another deep breath, grounding your energy into your body. Take one last deep breath, open your eyes, and blow out your candle.

Setting Up an Altar to 1111 and Archangel Sandalphon

If you don't have a wishing jar, now is the time to get one, as this will be the best thing to place upon your wish altar. Your wishing jar can look like anything you want, such as a genie lamp, a chalice, a spell box, a cup, or even a small piggy bank. The only requirement is that you can feed it your wishes. Your wishes can be on small slips of paper or sticky notes. Other things you will need for your altar include a picture of Sandalphon or an oracle card with his image on it, a gold or yellow candle to represent divine abundance, 1111 written on a yellow piece of paper, some salt, a pinch of dirt, some feathers, and anything else you feel you want to place upon the altar. You will also want to sit down and compose a prayer or intention statement to Sandalphon and 1111. An example might be: "Sandalphon, I call upon you to bless my wish, to carry it to the Divine and hand it off to the person responsible for making my wish come true."

Once you have your altar set up, I recommend spraying it with a sage spray or giving it a once-over with an abundance bundle smoke wand. These bundles generally consist of rosemary, juniper, and orange peel. This smoke will not only cleanse your altar, it will set the abundance energy tone for your wish.

Once your altar is clean, set, and ready for your prayer work, take a couple of nice deep breaths, light your candle, and speak your intention statement out loud, beginning with the words: "I call on Archangel Sandalphon and the power of 1111 to hear my intention, to assist me in achieving it in the most magical way. May my intention be for my higher good and the good of all those who may be involved in bringing it into reality." Then, go ahead and read your intention statement/prayer: "My intention/ prayer is ..."

To end the ritual, you can either blow the candle out or leave it burning if it is safe to do so. If you choose to blow your candle out, repeat these words first: "As I blow this candle out, I trust that its smoke carries my intention up to the heavens to be manifested by the Universe. I am ready to receive my asking, and so it is." Now, blow out your candle.

Once you have done your wish ritual on your altar, see yourself receiving your wish. Visualize Sandalphon bringing your wish fully fulfilled. See yourself being open and receptive with a smile on your face and waves of gratitude in your heart.

Automatic Writing Prompts

After you have done your prayer work, or even after you have done the visualization, you may notice that Sandalphon is dropping all sorts of hints, clues, and messages around your wish. These may come in the form of single words, sentences, or even just an inner knowing. If you feel moved to, pull out your journal and capitalize on this connection. Title your page "Talks with Sandalphon and the Vibrational Energy Known as 1111." If you are familiar with journal work, go ahead and start writing, as you will know how to feel the nudges of the information as it flows from the number 1111 and Archangel Sandalphon. If you are new to journaling, consider using the writing prompts below to get you started with the process:

1. Sandalphon, how will I know when you are around and what signs will you leave me?

2. Where in my life are miracles taking place that I may not be noticing?

3. Why have I struggled in the past to connect with the miracles in my everyday life?

4. How can I become more aware of the way I create miracles with my family, my coworkers, or my partner?

5. How will stepping into the energy of 1111 assist me today?

Use your journal to keep a working record of all the hints, nudges, and breadcrumbs Sandalphon leaves you. You just never know when one of them might be the key to yet another wish! The more I work with Sandalphon and the more I release, the more he likes to hint at what else is on offer if I am brave enough to wish again. So start to open, keep up the automatic writing, and let the wishes roll in.

Angel Crystal: Moonstone

Making a wish is akin to asking for a new beginning. Wishes bring in new energy. They open up doors that we thought were sealed or closed and bring with them potential for unknown possibilities. This new energy births all sorts of unknowns into our life, which makes moonstone the perfect stone to ground the energy of 1111 into. Moonstone will help you connect more deeply with the intuitive hints and signs Archangel Sandalphon will bring into your life. It will also assist you in trusting that what is unfolding is all part of your wish being manifested into the physical realm. In order to charge your moonstone and recode it with the frequency of 1111, you will need the following magic tools: a pocket-sized moonstone, a piece of paper, a pen, tape or a rubber band, a white or light blue candle for focus and communication, and a picture that represents your current wish. This could be a printout of your Pinterest page, a series of images pasted on a mood board, or just a single photo. Once you have all of your magical tools gathered, you will want to consult your moon phase calendar. For this activation, you need to pick a phase of the moon that feels right to you. This is where you will need to trust your gut, which is part and parcel to the frequency of 1111 to be honest.

Once you have selected what moon phase you are going to activate your moonstone under, it is time to prep your magical tools and get your Sandalphon altar ready for your ritual. On your piece of paper, write out your wish in as much detail as possible in the center of the paper. You can start with, "1111 and Archangel Sandalphon, I am claiming this wish ..." Place your wish. Now, draw a big heart around your wish, and then around the heart write as many 1111s as you can. Make sure you get at least eleven onto the paper or around the heart. Now, place the image of your wish into the center and place your moonstone on top of it. Fold your paper around your moonstone, making it a little parcel. You can seal it with tape or a rubber band. It is totally up to you.

Next, you will place this onto your Sandalphon altar along with your candle. If you feel called to add other items to your altar before you begin charging the crystal, go right ahead. This is your sacred space, and you can set it up any way you like. Remember not to start this ritual until the sun has set and the moon is up. Alternatively, you could do this very early in the morning while the moon is still high in the sky, before sunrise. Now you have your moon, your altar, and your moonstone wrapped and ready to go. Go ahead and light your candle. Sit back and place your hand on your heart and take nice, deep, slow breaths as you watch the flame dance. When you feel steady and fully present in the moment, repeat this simple script:

> *Under the power of the moon I lay my stone*
> *to charge its energy and to hear my call.*
> *The power of 1111 fills this stone,*
> *coding its layers and making it strong.*
> *When this candle sparks out, I know it will be done.*
> *Wishes fulfilled and energy anew,*
> *from angels' wings, the moon to me.*
> *What is written and blessed will come to be.*

Now, leave your candle to burn as long as it is safe to do so. If it is not, then go ahead and blow it out, but do your best to leave it as long as possible. Leave your stone on the altar until your moon phase is completed; normally that's about two and half days. Then unwrap your stone and start carrying it around with you until your wish comes to pass. You can place your paper and your picture up on your fridge or notice board so you can have reminders around your house or even put them in your wish jar on your altar, removing them only once the wish is complete. Once your wish is complete, you will want to clear your moonstone by either cleansing it with some sage or palo santo or laying it on a salt brick. Then it will be ready to be coded with your next wish.

Additional Numbers for Working with Sandalphon's Energy

1110—Wishes are unlimited, and there is no lack of them. When you see this number, you will be reminded that you can never make too many wishes. You can never ask for too much. Just follow your heart and fire your wishes off into the universe.

1112—Make a wish for your spouse, romantic partner, or business partner. Sharing your wishes with those you love will amplify your wishing energy and power.

1113—It is time to turn up the fun with your wishing power. Think of something that is playful, exciting, and you would want to invite all of your friends to come and enjoy. That wish is deep in the beats of your heart. Let it out and let your hair down.

1114—Sometimes it is good to make small wishes—simple, mundane wishes that only mean something to you. Not everything in your life has to be a grand gesture. Sometimes small and simple is just the right amount of magic to bring a smile to your face and a spring to your step.

1115—Wishes bring change with them. Like it or not, the wishes you are broadcasting have change embedded into them. So when you see this number, know that you have the power to ask specifically for the change you wish to see in your life, in your day, in your community, and in your world.

1116—Your heart knows what you truly want. It knows what you crave, and it knows what you need. When this number comes walking into your day, let your heart make a wish for something it knows you need.

1117—Wishes tend to bring lessons with them. They do not show up without something unknown and something to learn. This means that there is something in one of your wishes for you to know that you did not know before. Be on the lookout today for new information, new ideas, and new lessons coming to you with a wish fulfilled.

1118—One of your wishes is about to become manifest in the world of physical things, which means you must prepare for its arrival. Make space for it to show up, clear your mind of any doubt, and remove any lingering fear you may have about all the unknowns this wish will bring with it.

1119—Wishes can bring things to an end. They can bring about the end of a cycle, an end of a phase, or even the end of a journey. Something in your life is coming to an end, and it is just the wish your heart desired in order for you to move on to something more expansive and joyful.

1212 ~ ARCHANGEL ZADIKIEL
Use Appreciation to Expand into Ascension

"Appreciation shifts your energy and aligns you
with the frequencies of abundance. The more
we find to appreciate, the more we manifest
from a place of ascended awareness."

Deeper Meaning of 1212

The angel number 1212 wants you to connect to the moment,
to where you stand, sit, or lie right now as you read this. Here is
where the magic happens, in the moment you are in. Archangel
Zadikiel wants you to ground into the present, to stop and bring
your focus and attention to all that makes this moment, this second, everything it is. What had to conspire in your favor to make
this moment happen? Oftentimes we find ourselves so caught up

in our past or immersed in all the potential of the future that we forget that the fast path to expansion and ascension is in the here and now. The angel number 1212 is that reminder. It is the sign you need to stop, look around you, acknowledge where you are, and claim all that you appreciate about the present moment. As you look around, say out loud what it is you can claim. Appreciate your breath, your body, your functioning brain, the clothes protecting your skin, the food that provides the fuel for your physical vessel, and the body that moves and creates momentum.

Zadikiel is all about the here and now and about what is and what you have, for he knows it is the fastest path to what you want, need, and desire. He also understands you might not associate the word "rampage" with something creative and good, but anything that gets your blood pumping, engages all of you, and ignites your desire for momentum is wildly divine. In this context, rampage is used in a way to spark you up and get you excited about your life. The angel number 1212 wants to light a fire inside you and wants to get you up and moving. It wants to push you into top gear and do it where you are and with what you have at your disposal right now. The promise of the future is all around you. The dust of the past needs to be moved and cleaned away. All of this takes movement, it takes action, and it takes a rampage. The best way to get into the energy that 1212 wants you to create is to just start listing what is in your field of vision. Say, "I appreciate ..." and then start listing items you can see. The more you get into this naming of things to appreciate, the more you will find around you to appreciate.

Before you know it, you will have created such a strong vortex of energy that you will notice a physical shift in your body, and your mind will suddenly be on the search for even more things to appreciate. You will fire up parts of your brain that will be in desperate need to find more and more appreciative thoughts and feelings to connect to. This is how you build momentum and create a rampage of appreciation. This is the magic of 1212, and this is the gift that Archangel Zadikiel wants to bring into your life.

The Angel Zadikiel

When I first met Zadikiel, he was in the form of a bear and went by the name of Zeke, which is what I still call him. The bear was a guide of one of my friends, who, by the way, had no idea her bear was an angel. That realization came much, much later. I still remember almost wetting myself with laughter when she finally put two and two together. Zeke works with my friend in bear form as a healer, which is not really how we normally associate Zadikiel's energy. Honestly, appreciation is pretty damn healing. For when we are in the flow of appreciation, our entire radiant body changes, glows, and lights up the room. In other words, our life energy gets pumped up. The fact that Zadikiel, or Zeke as we in our house call him, can change form and actually prefers to shape-shift shows just how transformative the energy of appreciation can be. It literally transmutes and changes energy both in us and around us, which kind of makes the art of appreciation a shape-shifting superpower.

Zeke is often called the "angel of freedom and mercy," gifted with the ability to bless those who ask for God's mercy and forgiveness. This aligns Zeke with the ability to relieve one's suffering. Funnily enough, rampages of appreciation do the exact same thing. They move you out of the energy of suffering and ascend you into an energy of freedom, strength, and power. When the weighty shackles of pain, doubt, and sadness are broken, one feels lighter and full of life. This is what we refer to in energy work as expansion as opposed to contraction. More negative emotions, thoughts, and behaviors have a contracting effect on one's aura and energetic bodies. When we call on Zeke, he helps us uncoil and to slowly, gently, and lovingly expand. He does all of this through the power of 1212 and the art of appreciation. This is magic medicine for our body, mind, and spirit. So no matter what form Zeke shows up to you in, just know that he is there to shape-shift your vibes. He is scrubbing up and ready to give you a new glow, one that starts on the inside. This treatment is totally pain- and drug-free. All you have to do is start listing things you appreciate. Just a thought, but maybe start with Zeke.

Visualization/Meditation from Zadikiel: Align to Appreciation Vibes

This meditation is designed to assist you in aligning with the frequency of appreciation. The more you do this meditation, the more aligned to the vibrational frequency of appreciation you will be. You see, appreciation isn't something you just do once every so often; it is a vortex of energy, a spinning wheel of vibrational energy that you can live in 24/7. Make sure you do this meditation somewhere quiet and where you will not be disturbed. If you feel called to, you can light a purple candle to connect your third eye and crown chakra and have it burning throughout the meditation. Just remember to blow it out once you are done. You can record this script and listen to it so you can close your eyes, or you can simply keep your eyes open and read through the words. Either way, you will connect with energy and it will benefit you.

Do what is most comfortable for you.

Let us begin.

Go ahead and get comfortable; find a relaxing yoga pose or a comfy seat and just focus on your breath, breathing in through the nose and out through the mouth. With each breath, allow your body to relax. Drop the shoulders, feeling the tension release from the back of your neck, and allow a wave of relaxation to wash over you from the top of your head to the tips of your toes. As you continue breathing in and out, allowing this relaxing wave of energy to wash over you, you may feel inclined to close your eyes and sink deeper and deeper into this calm and peaceful space. As you breathe in and out, continue to let this wave of relaxation flow over you. Once you feel as relaxed as you can get, call in the energy of Archangel Zadikiel. Ask him to step forward in any form he chooses. Just stay open to feeling his presence with you, letting his energy into this wave of relaxed energy. Feel the energy that is flowing from the top of your head to the tips of your toes as it becomes infused with Zadikiel's love, support, and guidance.

As you breathe and allow Archangel Zadikiel into your energy field, grant him permission to infuse your aura as you place your fingers on your forehead between your brow points on the third eye. Ever so gently, press on this spot as you say the following intention statements:

I am the frequency of appreciation.

Press in and breathe.

I am surrounded by the frequency of appreciation.

Gently press and breathe in and out, imprinting these intention statements into your mind through the third eye.

The frequency of appreciation flows through me and around me.

The frequency of appreciation moves through every aspect of my life.

Impress and breathe.

I breathe this frequency of appreciation in, and I breathe this frequency out.

I am the frequency of appreciation, I am.

Inhale, exhale, and press this onto your mind. Impress this energy of appreciation deep into your consciousness.

Inhale, exhale, impress the energy of Archangel Zadikiel into your mind, into your vibration, and deep into your consciousness.

Breathe.

Slowly take your fingers away from your third eye, giving yourself a moment to stay in this beautiful, relaxed energy as you feel this frequency of appreciation, this new angelic energy, become part of your aura and part of your vibrational being. As you continue to inhale and exhale this vibrational frequency of appreciation into your body, thank Archangel Zadikiel for being with you today. Know without a doubt that as you bring your focus back to the room and back to your body, his energy is now impressed into your mind, your body, your aura, and your vibrational field. Everywhere you go and everything you do will be infused with this frequency of appreciation and the energy of the archangels.

Give yourself a moment to become fully aware, fully present, and fully focused. Take your time as you slowly open your eyes and prepare yourself for the rest of your day or your evening slumber.

Setting Up an Altar to 1212 and Archangel Zadikiel

Appreciation is one of those things that happens in the moment. It is a here-and-now energy and your altar should represent that. Although similar to gratitude and blessings, appreciation is more an honoring energy. When we want to honor how something is, we appreciate it. So what is it you want to honor with Archangel Zadikiel? This could be a person in your life, a place that makes you feel alive, or a job that you love. Grab some items that represent what it is you want to honor. You may even want to make a small vision or mood board to represent what you are honoring. Once it is finished, place it on your altar. Other things you will need for your altar include a picture of Zadikiel or an oracle card that has Zadikiel on it, a pink candle for the heart chakra, 1212 written on a pink piece of paper, some salt for protection, a pinch of dirt to ground your prayer, some feathers for the angels, and anything else you feel you want to place upon the altar. You will also want to sit down and compose a prayer or intention statement to Zadikiel and 1212. An example might be: "Zadikiel, I place these items on my altar as a form of appreciation for what I have in my life. I honor this person, place, or thing right now in this moment as they are and for how they make me feel right here, right now. Thank you, Zadikiel, for offering me this sacred space to honor what is right in front of me."

Once you have your altar set up, I recommend giving it a quick cleanse with the smoke of an herb bundle or some clearing spray made with essential oils. This cleansing is part of your altar magic and sets the tone of your appreciation ritual. When your altar is ready, take a couple of deep breaths, light your candle, and speak your intention statement out loud, beginning with the words: "I call on Archangel Zadikiel and the power of 1212 to hear my intention, to assist me in achieving it in the most blessed way. May my intention be for my higher good and the good of all those who may be involved in bringing this intention into reality." Then go ahead and read your intention statement/prayer: "My intention/prayer is…"

To end the ritual, you can either blow the candle out or leave it burning if it is safe to do so. If you choose to blow your candle out, repeat these words first: "As I blow this candle out, I trust that its smoke carries my intention up to the heavens to be manifested by the Universe. I am ready to receive my asking, and so it is." Now, blow out your candle.

Automatic Writing Prompts

Now that you have had time to connect with Archangel Zadikiel throughout this chapter via meditation and prayer work, you may notice you are starting to see evidence of Zeke's energy around you. You may have been feeling nudges, hearing whispers, or even just noticing hints or nudges from the angels. Messages are coming in and waiting for you to engage with them. These messages may come in the form of single words, sentences, or even just an inner knowing. To capitalize on this connection you are establishing with Archangel Zadikiel, grab your journal and start diving into some automatic writing. Title your page "Talks with Zadikiel and the Vibrational Energy Known as 1212." If you are familiar with journaling work, go ahead and start writing, as you will know how to feel the nudges of the information as it flows from the number 1212 and Archangel Zadikiel. If you are new to journal work, consider using the writing prompts below to get you started with the process:

1. Zadikiel, how will I know when you are around?

2. Where should I start my rampage of appreciation today?

3. Why have I struggled in the past to bring the energy of appreciation into my life?

4. How can I use your shape-shifting abilities to transform any fear and resistance I have around being appreciative of my life and all that is in it?

5. How will stepping into the energy of 1212 assist me today?

You may find that the prompts themselves get you into a nice writing flow, and before you know it, you have moved beyond them. Just lean into the process, trust that Zadikiel is guiding your hand, and do not try to make logical sense of anything that comes up initially.

Angel Crystal: Larimar

This beautiful, almost angelic, blue crystal helps open up the throat chakra while drawing energy up from your heart. It is said to bring about a sense of peace, calm, joy, and compassion when it is either held or worn. That makes it a perfect stone to work with as you learn to speak the love you have for your life and rant your way to appreciation ascension, which in turn makes larimar the ideal crystal to ground the energy of 1212 and Archangel Zadikiel. To code your crystal to the frequency of 1212 and embed Zadikiel's energy into it, you will need the following magical tools: a pen, a pocket-size larimar crystal, pictures of people, animals, or things you appreciate, tape or a rubber band,

and a white candle (a tea light will work just fine). You will also need to grab a calendar and find out when your next first quarter moon is, as you want to code your crystal when the moon is in balance but still growing. This balanced—but still expanding—energy is part of the appreciation 1212 energy you wish to embed into your crystal.

Once you have all of your magical tools and know when the next first quarter moon is, get your paper and pen and draw a heart as large as the paper itself. Inside the heart, write 1212 and then place your pictures over the top, putting your crystal in the center. Now, wrap it up in a neat little bundle and secure it with either some tape or the rubber band. Take this to your Zadikiel altar or any other altar you feel inclined to and light your candle. Once your candle is lit, place your hand on your heart and take a couple of deep, slow breaths, inhaling through the nose and exhaling through the mouth. Use the breath work as a way to tune in and connect your body and mind to the moment. When you feel focused and centered, call in Archangel Zadikiel and ask him to use the power of the first quarter moon to code the frequency of 1212 and appreciation into your crystal. You can use a prayer, an affirmation, or write up an intention statement if you feel inclined to, but it is not necessary. Stay within the energy for as long as you feel you need to, but no shorter than two minutes. If possible, let the candle burn all the way down and leave your crystal on the altar for an additional forty-eight hours. Once done, unwrap and carry it with you either in your pocket or your bra or place it in your bag. If, however, you infused a pendant or bracelet, you can now wear it as a reminder to appreciate each and every moment of your day knowing that you have the ability to shape-shift your energy, your thoughts, your feelings, and your life.

Additional Numbers for
Working with Zadikiel's Energy

1210—It is time to appreciate the wonder of all the unknown possibilities in your life. There is so much untapped potential around you right now. Speak it into being and allow it to be.

1211—Give yourself permission to toot your own horn today. Make a list of things you have done well this week, including big wins, small wins, and places where you stepped up and led through the act of appreciation.

1213—It's time to off-load your appreciation rants on your friends, as someone in your life needs to know how important they are to you and how much you appreciate having them in your orbit.

1214—Now is the time to create a money-catching account. Use it to save your change and allow it to be one of the ways you show your appreciation for always being surrounded by abundance. If you already have one, pat yourself on the back for being so incredible with your manifesting energy.

1215—Acts of appreciation cause change. Look around you, as you have changed not only yourself but the energy of the immediate world around you.

1216—Your family needs to know how much you appreciate them. Find a way today to honor your family, be it biological or self-made, and let everyone soak up the appreciation vibes.

1217—Rejoice in your knowledge and wisdom today. No matter how you attained it, it has served you well. Do a rampage of appreciation for your brain, your knowledge, and your expertise.

1218—No matter your circumstances, there is something physical in your life you deeply appreciate. It could be something small, or it could be something large. It doesn't matter what it is. Write it a love song, give it a kiss, and allow yourself to get lost in your appreciation for it.

1219—There are so many things to appreciate when something comes to an end. Find it today and cling to that instead of allowing your mind to hook into what is being left behind.

CONCLUSION

Over the course of this book, you have been introduced to thirteen archangels. You have taken a journey with them and invited them into your life, but you don't have to stop your work with them once you put this book away. My hope is that you form a bond with at least one of the angels you have worked with and that you keep one of the angel altars up in your home and learn to call in that angel to support and guide you. Whether that angel becomes your new meditation mat buddy or your safe space for prayer, the angel, or angels, you bonded with in this book want to help. They want to be part of your joy, happiness, health, and well-being. They want to love you, shower you with miracles, and bless you each and every day. However, they can only do that if you allow them to. This book is not only an introduction; it has also been an invitation from the angels to spend more time with them, a reminder that they are there with you at all times and that they want nothing more than to be of service to you. Before you put this book away or back on your bookshelf, make sure you have sent an RSVP to the angels or the angel of your choosing and let them know you accept them and their offer of assistance, blessings, and vibrational energy into your life.

Well, dear reader, our time together has come to an end. The angels and I thank you for spending this time with us, and we want you to know that we are always happy to connect with you. We would also love to see you at one of our live angel channeling events. Just ask to join our Quantum Wealth Collective for Luxe Goddess Entrepreneurs Group on Facebook, as we would love to stay connected. Until then, may you walk with the angels and create miracles with each and every step you take.

And so it is.

Blessed be.

To Write to the Author

If you wish to contact the author or would like more information about this book, please write to the author in care of Llewellyn Worldwide Ltd. and we will forward your request. Both the author and publisher appreciate hearing from you and learning of your enjoyment of this book and how it has helped you. Llewellyn Worldwide Ltd. cannot guarantee that every letter written to the author can be answered, but all will be forwarded. Please write to:

Leeza Robertson
⅄ Llewellyn Worldwide
2143 Wooddale Drive
Woodbury, MN 55125-2989

Please enclose a self-addressed stamped envelope for reply,
or $1.00 to cover costs. If outside the U.S.A., enclose
an international postal reply coupon.

Many of Llewellyn's authors have websites with additional information and resources. For more information, please visit our website at http://www.llewellyn.com.